CO-AKZ-983

An Ideal Betrayed

TESTIMONIES OF A PROMINENT
AND LOYAL MEMBER OF THE
SOVIET ESTABLISHMENT

Mikhail Nenashev

OPEN GATE PRESS
LONDON

FLORIDA STATE
UNIVERSITY LIBRARIES

JUN 25 2001

TALLAHASSEE, FLORIDA

First published in English in 1995 by Open Gate Press
51 Achilles Road, London NW6 1DZ

Originally published in Russian
by Progress Publishing Group, Moscow,
entitled *A Hostage of our Times*.

Translated into English by Progress Publishing Group.
Copyright © 1992 and 1994 by Mikhail Nenashev
Edited translation © Open Gate Press 1995
All rights reserved.

British Library Cataloguing-in-Publication Programme
A catalogue record for this book is available from the British Library

ISBN: 1 871871 25 5

DK
290.3
.N46
A3
1995

FLORIDA STATE
UNIVERSITY LIBRARIES

3 1254 03528 5911

JUN 25 2001

TALLAHASSEE, FLORIDA

Printed in Great Britain by
Cromwell Press, Melksham, Wiltshire

Table of Contents

Glossary and list of useful dates   v

Preface to the English Edition   vii

Chapter 1 – Beginnings   1

Chapter 2 – At Work in the Party   14

    The Provincial Party: Its Form and Functioning   14

    The Party Centre: Staraya Square and Its Inhabitants   26

    The Betrayal and Death of the CPSU   40

Chapter 3 – 'Sweet Hell': Eight Years at *Sovetskaya*
               Rossiya   47

    Getting Started   47

    The Editor's Sweet Sorrow   53

Chapter 4 – The Publishing Business: My Last Love   65

    A Sense of Futility: The Commercialisation of
               Publishing   73

Chapter 5 – A Chance Missed: In the USSR Committee
               for Television and Radio   79

    The Unfathomable World of Television   81

    Chairman of Gosteleradio   92

    The Spiritual Mission of Television   105

Chapter 6 – Illusions of Freedom   117

    The Heavy Burden of a Loyal Performer   117

    Perestroika: The Betrayal of People's Hopes   124

Chapter 7 – 'Thou Shalt Not Create Idols':
               The Tragedy of Gorbachev's Supporters   133

Glossary and list of useful dates

CC CPSU	Central Committee of the Communist Party of the Soviet Union
Goskomizdat	USSR State Committee for Publishing, Printing and Book Trading
Gosteleradio	USSR State Committee for Television and Radio
NKVD	People's Commissariat for Internal Affairs
RSFSR	Russian Soviet Federative Socialist Republic (Russia's name while part of the Soviet Union)
VAAP	USSR Copyright Agency

20th CPSU Conference	February 1956
25th CPSU Conference	February 1976
27th CPSU Conference	February 1986
29th CPSU Conference	Nov-Dec 1991

19th Party Conference	July 1988

1st Congress of People's Deputies	June 1990
6th Congress of People's Deputies	April 1992
7th Congress of People's Deputies	December 1992
8th Congress of People's Deputies	March 1993

Preface to the English Edition

Books, like people, have their own history, their own identity and purpose. The purpose of this book is to present to the reader some of the thoughts and testimonies of a man whom fate guided to the very heights of party and state authority in the USSR: a member of the Central Committee of the Communist Party and minister in the last Soviet government.

Russia remains the focus of public opinion, for it dictates to a large extent the course of events in modern-day Europe and the world.

The more time that elapses since the disintegration of the USSR, the more intense the debate: was its ruin legitimate, an inevitable result of a natural historical process, or the product of the fateful mistakes of those who stood at the helm of power, those who, in 1985, launched the changes which they brashly termed perestroika? Were there other controllable, non-destructive ways for the country to switch over to market relations? Did the changes have to be accompanied by bloody national conflicts, the impoverishment of most of the population, the degradation of society, education, the sciences and arts? The questions go on...

We are not yet fully in a position to assess what happened to the USSR or to judge the country we have lost. The time for fundamental research has not yet come. But we can and must look at our recent past in order to identify the beginnings of Russia's present troubles and tragedies.

The past is unable to advise us about the present. It can only serve as a warning. This book is a warning to those who stand at the helm of power in today's Russia and who hold the key to the country's future.

Two years have passed since *An Ideal Betrayed* was written, and the author takes the liberty in this preface of recalling that his

vii

judgements of perestroika and the exploits of its leaders – Gorbachev and Yeltsin – have not lost their relevance and have been borne out by life itself.

There is no need here to return to the subject matter of the book itself. Suffice it to return to the dramatic events of 8th December 1991, when the leaders of three former Soviet republics – Boris Yeltsin, Leonid Kravchuk and Stanislav Shushkevich – took the decision to carve up the USSR. The three years which have passed since that historic moment have greatly enabled us to see the extent of the tragedy which it has caused.

Analysts from the Gorbachev Foundation have dedicated the book *The Union Could Have Been Preserved* to the event in question. In their discourse on the events leading up to the signing of the Belavezhskaya Pushcha accords, the authors say the event was merely a culmination of the national tragedy that had affected this great country and its people. At the presentation of the book in December 1994, Mikhail Gorbachev posed several questions which may be of interest: why have the peoples of the USSR, who sacrificed over 25 million lives in the name of their homeland during the Great Patriotic War of 1941-1945, lost their enormous state and monumental history? Why was it that Russian politicians initiated the disintegration of historical Russia? Why did the Russian parliament, filled with people who called themselves 'patriots', pronounce the death sentence on the country that was, during the last hundred years, called Russia, then Soviet Russia?

The above questions are most relevant, particularly for the citizens of the former USSR. However, while we think about them, we inevitably come to the conclusion that Gorbachev himself bears most of the responsibility for the disintegration of the USSR. He must answer for everything that took place in the state which he led and with which the people and history entrusted him.

Gorbachev's weakness and the inevitability of his downfall arose mainly from the fact that he was a man from the provinces and knew the Russia which he was entrusted to rule poorly. Let us not forget that this shortcoming was shared by others, too. Since the baptism of Rus over 800 years ago, all changes and transformations in our fatherland have been dictated from above, for example by Ivan the Terrible, Peter I and the Bolsheviks. Gorbachev and his predecessors did little to understand their country or identify its specific requirements and tried, with their reforms, to dress Russia in unfamiliar clothing and impose foreign ideals.

Gorbachev's political shortsightedness was evident, especially when he decided to reform, or rather destroy the state's political system and its main bastion, the Communist Party. The party, after decades of monopoly over power, lost much: the ability to conduct politics, support among the people, the capacity to understand the actual needs of the country. Yet it managed to preserve stability in the state. By destroying the party, Gorbachev was no longer able to govern such a complex multinational union as the USSR was.

To this end an attempt to judge the events of 19 August 1991 (the so-called attempted coup) objectively reveals that those events speeded up Gorbachev's fall and made it clear to all that he was no longer able to keep control. August 1991 also revealed Gorbachev's human weaknesses: he lacked the character of a real man and political will, was afraid of responsibility and decision-taking at a time when events were assuming threatening proportions for the country.

What the coup leaders said on the above during their investigation and trial is open to criticism. However, their unanimity that Gorbachev during those days was most of all afraid to make decisions must be remembered. He did not state, at our last meeting in Foros, with whom of those on the barricades in Moscow his loyalties lay. Gorbachev did not back his colleagues in their risky attempt to introduce a state of emergency, but he did nothing to oppose them and manifest himself as a true leader. With all due sympathy, it is still difficult to explain how, given the power at his disposal, including his status as supreme commander of the armed forces, Gorbachev was able to sit back under symbolic guard and wait with weak will to see how events would unfurl in the wake of the attempted coup. It is impossible to understand how the Soviet president was able to remain at a seaside resort while the country was being ruined, and wait to be collected and taken to Moscow to be told what he should do.

I must make it clear to the British reader that, as I explain in detail in my book, I am not one of those who zealously shift all of the blame on to Gorbachev. He was, though, the most to blame as leader, as the first leader on whom the outcome of events depended.

Moreover we, the members of his team in the Central Committee and in the government, have only learned in hindsight how properly to view Gorbachev. We did nothing to stop the state and party from being destroyed or overcome the shortcomings of our leader and free our state while it was not too late.

I do not conceal the fact that I am tormented by my own conscience and am aware of my own blame for the troubles and the losses that my country is now suffering. Our problem was that we were too quick to make Gorbachev out to be an idol and were caught up in mindless obedience. Perhaps this will seem offensive to some, but we supporters of Gorbachev, at a difficult time for our country, were like sheep in a flock which the shepherd had left exposed to a storm.

One other question may spring to the mind of the British reader, who may still think of Gorbachev as the man who freed Russia from the tyranny of the Bolsheviks: can Gorbachev and his party change anything today and influence a kind of rebirth of the USSR? The answer is no, for Gorbachev has no party in Russia and no supporters. There must be no illusion about this in the West. If Gorbachev and his followers were unable to act to save Russia, the Soviet Union, in 1991, they are even less likely to do so now.

Boris Yeltsin is Gorbachev's antipode not only in politics but also in his personal qualities. In contrast to Gorbachev, Yeltsin is a man of will, capable of taking even the most risky of decisions. One of those decisions, the most tragic of them, was to dissolve the USSR.

This was the final act in the struggle between Yeltsin and Gorbachev for power, where the object of destruction was power itself in the form of the state. A dramatic situation arose: Yeltsin was unable to become president of the USSR, and would have been unable to get round Gorbachev if the Soviet Union had been preserved. Power could be snatched from Gorbachev only by the most paradoxical but most natural method – liqudiating the USSR. That is what Yeltsin did.

For Russia, the Belavezhskaya Pushcha accords bore neither logic nor common sense. It is hard to think of another example from history whereby people thirsting for power purposefully destroyed the very foundation of that power – the state.

The struggle for power did not end there. One adversary was replaced by another – the Supreme Soviet, the parliament of Russia. It was precisely in that body that Yeltsin in 1993 saw the greatest threat to his power. Indeed the parliament had done all that the president wanted it to do, endowing him with all kinds of powers. However, as soon as the Supreme Soviet tried to plan an independent role and began to draw more public support, it became a source of danger for the president's sole command.

The events of the battle with the parliament are well known. I shall not dwell on the details – who issued the first shot outside Ostankino or the White House in October 1993 and so on. The important fact is that Yeltsin, by decree of September 21, signalled the beginning of a struggle for power by any means. That struggle did not end by cutting off electricity, water and central heating in the parliament building, which was cordoned off, or isolating the deputies. The cost of the conflict – power – was too high. The decree of September 21 was not about the dissolution of the parliament, but its elimination. But the majority of the nation did not support Yeltsin's decision, and the blockade swelled day by day with supporters of the Supreme Soviet.

Whatever the arguments in favour of the use of the armed forces on 3 October 1993, nothing can explain or justify the use of heavy tanks against the parliament and its supporters. The more time that has elapsed since the tragedy, the more frightening the scene, in front of all the witnesses, of how opponents are dealt with, when tanks, in broad daylight and in front of television cameras from all over the world, fired at unarmed people and the windows of the Supreme Soviet building in order to burn it to a cinder. The British reader should be well aware that the watered-down parliament that came into being after the elections to replace the old one is not strengthening state power but only weakening and making it unpredictable.

Much is written and spoken in the West of the danger of Zhirinovsky coming to power in Russia. I would like to mention that the lack of faith by many in Yeltsin and his supporters is the main detonator for potential explosions and the deformation of public awareness. The success of Zhirinovsky, whom many see as a fascist threat to society, was, in fact, only a manifestation of that mistrust and the gathering momentum of protest against those who seek power. It was a gesture of open opposition to misconceived experiments and reforms among all sections of the population.

We are able today to view the past in a different light. We condemn the Bolsheviks and Lenin, with his written instructions consisting of one word alone – 'shoot'. We stigmatise the tyranny of Stalin, under whom thousands met their death. But how are we to describe and judge those in power today, those who have consciously destroyed the historical core of Russia, who have broken the fundamental structure of the country's security and proclaimed sovereignty without bounds for all nations and regions and yet are today sending the tanks into little Chechnya?

And how are we to describe those who, with their policies, are consciously turning many millions of Russians into outcasts and potential refugees? Surely Yeltsin and those who were party to the destruction of the USSR knew that the separation of Russia, Ukraine, Belorussia, Central Asia and Kazakhstan would result in suffering for the millions of Russian-speaking people who have settled in those countries during the last hundred years.

Can common sense be used to explain the logic of those politicians? Or was there neither logic nor common sense behind their policies? What then drove them? The answer is this alone – the temptation of power. And that temptation was so great for Yeltsin and his allies, so great was their desire to occupy the Kremlin halls that the misfortunes of millions did not disturb them during their quest.

Russians are outraged and concerned most of all by the arbitrariness of corrupt officials. The new democratic official has already mastered and thrived in their art of bribe-taking, which was rife both in Soviet and Tsarist times. Enjoying unlimited power and lawlessness, today's Russian official relates to the ordinary Russian as a victor to the vanquished, acting at will and settling scores. Corruption in the government administration is now ubiquitous. Top officials from among the old party structures and new democrats are selling the nation's wealth wholesale and retail, permitting only those able and prepared to express gratitude to take a slice of the proceeds. As a result, Russia is set to become a unique country in terms of redistribution of national wealth: today 90 per cent of the population own less than a half of all property, and the other half belongs to a mere 10 per cent of the population. It is not difficult to assume that sooner or later that large part of the population which has been robbed will take to the streets and demand a fresh distribution of property.

Personal gain in Russia today has absolute priority and prevails above state interests. Corruption and theft of various kinds are not only wrong, not only do they deprave society, but are costly for the nation, for they push consumer prices for goods up between 30 and 50 per cent. Criminal scientists are correct in saying that corruption is an integral part of internal policy, just as war, for example – only the nation itself inevitably becomes a victim of that policy.

By destroying the Communist system, radical democrats thought they could gain the opportunity to develop society along rational western lines. In fact in Russia's individual national circumstances, the radical nature of reforms, which did not conform with those circumstances, gave rise to an uncontrollable, extremely crime-ridden and corrupt process of dividing and redistributing property and power which was not along European lines, but more akin to what has happened in Latin America.

The reader may with all justification ask of me: if the present authorities do not enjoy the support of the majority of Russians, what, then, keeps them in power and helps them to retain control in such an enormous country?

I repeat once again that Yeltsin's easy, bloodless accession to power was linked with the full loss of faith by society in Gorbachev. The events of August 1991, which testified to the deep power crisis, created what were almost perfect conditions for a change in leadership.

Why, then, does the nation today so patiently bear its cross and reconcile itself with the arbitrariness of the leadership amid Yeltsin's clear inability to govern Russia and stop the process of economic, political and spiritual degradation of the country? There can be only one answer – the current top echelons of power have been amazingly fortunate in inheriting a mass of people whom the CPSU – through its own enormous fault – deprived of political will during the many years of mindless obedience.

There is one other question which I cannot leave unanswered. Is not the fate of the USSR simply a favourable outcome to a scenario written by the West and which meets the West's interests? That opinion is widespread among the Russian public today. I believe that if such a scenario had, in fact, been written, then it could have been enacted in some other country. But in such a huge area as Russia no scenario amounts to more than idle speculation, and the action can take place only if it corresponds with the plans and interests of internal social and political parties, movements and groups. It is another matter that the rules of that scenario may indeed coincide with those plans.

My assertion by no means exempts the West from any involvement in the current fate of Russia. It has been firmly established that some powerful western circles wanted to see Russia weakened as much as possible. The truth, moreover, that those circles were unprepared for the complex problems which arose when the geopolitical equilibrium which used to exist in the world was undermined must not be overlooked. It is obvious today that the most feasible option for rational people in the West would be for the USSR to be reborn on a new basis.

Nobody is able to predict the course of events in Russia today, for they are not guided by ordinary logic. However, it sufficiently fair to assert that democracy is unable to develop under the present authorities. It is becoming clearer and clearer that those who consider that democracy can gain the right conditions for its own assertion only if the current president leaves the Kremlin and the Kremlin is occupied by a decision-taking parliament are right. Power held by one man over a country so vast, which has no democratic traditions and which is faced by complex social and national problems, will inevitably transform the consciousness of any politician and turn him into a dictator.

The prospects for Russia's democratic movement are very grim, but, by and large, obvious. The reader must understand that the complexity of the situation in which Yeltsin finds himself today lies also in the fact that there is nowhere for him to go after leaving his highest post. It is very doubtful that a new president who comes to power on the crest of the general exposure of the current regime and who inherits a destroyed and plundered country would permit

Yeltsin to calmly spend the rest of his days in a foundation similar to that of Gorbachev. One of a new president's first steps would be to declare Yeltsin and his closest supporters guilty of causing the misfortunes and tragedies which Russia is suffering.

Power, like youth, is carefree and self-assured and does not like to draw lessons from its predecessors. My generation of the sixties, which came to believe sincerely in Gorbachev's perestroika, suffered defeat, although we had enough courage, common sense and dignity to admit that defeat and yield power to our successors. Do the current authorities in Russia, who have brought the country to the edge of an abyss, have the same courage to admit defeat and yield peacefully? Judging by the development of events in Russia today, especially in the Caucasus, that is open to question. And there will inevitably be further tragedies, which will bring my Fatherland new trouble and suffering.

Mikhail Nenashev
December 1994

Chapter 1 – Beginnings

My parents were simple, ordinary folk. They were of peasant stock, the roots of which were lost in central Russia, in Tambov Province. Before they were born (only a year separated the two, my father being born in 1908 and my mother in 1909), their own parents had settled in Orenburg Province, in search of a better life, in the Cossack settlement of Borodinovka in the Berezinovskaya stanitsa. There, in November 1929, I was born. My grandfather on my father's side, Yakov Nenashev, was a non-commissioned Cossack officer, and my grandfather on my mother's side, Andrei Trufanov, was a cavalry sergeant-major and had won two George Crosses during the Russo-Japanese war in 1905.

The family in which my mother was born and grew up was poor. My grandfather and his brothers spent most of their lives (apart from their years of compulsory Cossack service and the wars in defence of the Tsar and Fatherland) labouring and living on the estates of rich Cossacks. They were well known as shepherds and skilful horsemen. I was able to judge that for myself when, just five years old, Grandfather Andrei sat me on a horse for the first time and I fell off at once like a sackful. Grandfather, hiding his disappointment, patiently demonstrated how a true Cossack should conduct himself on horseback.

My father's family was prosperous, but only because they worked in the fields from dawn to dusk and had a solid farmstead with their own horses and oxen. My father would describe how they – three brothers and two sisters – had worked from childhood without rest days on their land. Yet the dividends were evidently not particularly high, as all three brothers, my father, the youngest of them recalled, wore one and the same coat and boots when they married, although eight years separated eldest from youngest.

My mother, from a lowly family of farm-labourers, which still lived in its cottage, dug into the ground with a floor made of straw, when she got married, was one of 13 children. Of them, only three survived – the eldest brother Vasily, Stepan and my mother herself. The others died of illness and disease. In 1919, at the height of the civil war, whipped up first by the Whites and then by the Reds, Vasily died in the grassy Orenburg steppes. In 1921, a year of famine in the Urals, when over a third of the village died, Stepan went to the closest town of Troitsk to find bread. He exchanged the remains of his Cossack clothing for a bucket of flour, was late returning with his 'riches' and spent the night at a farmstead by the roadside. The owners, thoroughly unpleasant people, saw what their guest was carrying, killed him during the night and threw his body far from the house. And so, my mother became her parents' last and only hope and joy.

My father was one of nine children, of whom only three brothers and two sisters remained alive. Being the youngest, father had to live with his parents and care for them until the end of their days, according to peasant tradition. It so happened, but that peasant tradition had little role to play. In 1937, the district NKVD (People's Commissariat for Internal Affairs) arrested all brothers, my father included, and even grandfather (their father). It was February, the height of the mass campaign to root out enemies of the people in every village, town and city, from Moscow to the farthest-flung regions. I remember those arrests well. They happened at night. Like a merciless scythe on grass, they came upon many a family. My father and grandfather were released after a few months. They were not sent from the district centre to remote places only because, I suppose, the quota for arrests in our district had been over-fulfilled or because there were not enough long-distance rail cars to take all the arrested away. I cannot think of any other reasons.

My father's eldest brother Ivan and the next one Yakov simply vanished. We received no letters from them and they were post-humously rehabilitated only in 1956. My father, after chancing to avoid the same fate, lived most of his life under the stigma of enemy of the people and in constant fear for his children (there were four of us) and with the added responsibility for father's own parents and the many children his brothers had left.

When I grew up I often wondered how my father found the

strength to survive that burden, seemingly impossible for one person alone to bear, and the years of unremitting fear for himself and his closest ones. Yet he never dwelt on this theme, undertaking once and for all not to rub salt into open wounds and wanting to guard us, his children, from circumstances linked with his past which could be dangerous.

My own childhood was not as splendid as the classic writers make a childhood out to be. My clearest memories were not of the sun rising above the far limits of the village early in the morning, nor the evening dew on the forest edge, but the constant struggle for survival. For an ordinary country family life itself, daily routine was all about the search for bread. I was the eldest of the children and had more responsibility. A peasant's cares are many and endless all year round: to grow and harvest a big plot of land, without which it was impossible to survive; to make hay and feed the cow and sheep; to prepare fuel for the long Urals winter; and many other tasks all came my way together with the adults. I remember how my mother, taking pity on me and in a bid to break the monotony of weeding the plot of land all summer, repeated the words: 'The eyes are afraid but the hands do the work.' Does that all mean that I had a difficult childhood, or was it just an ordinary country childhood, like that of all my contemporaries? The latter, I think, was true. Childhood contained more happiness than misery, as should be the case at that age, and those days were long and memorable, unlike the present days.

The war changed much, leaving nobody untouched. Duly, it conditioned my own young fate. The school in our village, which had been working as a seven-year school for only a few years, had closed down, with nobody to teach and nobody to do the teaching. In autumn 1941 I travelled to the district centre with my contemporaries to continue my education in the fifth year.

The years of war and study were difficult, and constantly troubled, because every month we had to see our relatives off to the front. Hardly a day passed without receiving news of the dead at the front. The school itself was remarkable in those years firstly in that its main building in the district centre housed a hospital, secondly in that it was located in old village homes in five places, and thirdly in that the male teachers had left for the front and there

3

were not enough teachers for many subjects. Those years were remarkable too for their constant feeling of hunger, for there was often simply nothing to eat. Hunger in all those war years was often accompanied by cold because we were not properly dressed and there was nobody to prepare firewood for the school (we had to do that ourselves). The school of the war years was unable to enhance our knowledge but, to be fair, it did teach us the meaning of life, the severity of which was itself a wise teacher, whose lessons we remembered always.

A number of new terms were introduced in those years, such as politotdel (a political department) (these were set up in the war years in state farms and machine and tractor stations), raikom (a district committee) and NKVD. I first learned of the NKVD in the winter of 1937 as something sinister, capable of taking our father away for ever and even that humble existence to which we were accustomed. The large wooden district NKVD building was situated close to the dug-out which my aunty (father's sister) called home and in which I lived when I went to school in the district centre. Every day, as I passed the building, its windows always covered by thick curtains, I often wondered what secrets could lie within. I was unable to understand much at the time but, like a small animal, I felt by instinct that there was nothing good about the building, that it was dangerous for myself and many others.

2

Student years are special years for all. In autumn 1948 I entered the History Faculty of the Magnitogorsk Pedagogical Institute. Magnitogorsk – because it was the nearest institute around, only a hundred kilometres from our district centre. The fact that I chose both a pedagogical institute and a history faculty was no accident, since I had loved the humanities and literature since childhood.

Looking back, the Magnitogorsk Pedagogical Institute was, even compared to the other provincial institutes with all their short-comings, one of the worst. Built during the steel works construction boom in 1933 and lifeless during the war years, it stood out in 1948 for its indescribable mediocrity and poverty. The assembly hall, evidently the institute's best hall at one time, was filled with ordinary park benches on iron supports. The hall, like many auditoriums, was, for all the years during which we studied, in a dangerous condition and had to be closed from time to time. In terms of teaching and qualification this institute met only the standards of a two-year teaching institute. In its first two years, its staff did not number one professor or doctor of science, and candidates of science were also a rarity in its faculties. It is easier today to assess the institute with hindsight than it was in 1948 when I, a shy first-year student, arriving in the city for the first time from the countryside after living there for all of my 18 years without seeing the outside world, entered the seat of learning. Reverently, and with provincial directness and timidity, I approached everything that the institute had to offer.

We students did not spend long at the very first stage of our course – two terms only. What, if anything, that got in the way of country school leavers was our shyness, the fear of looking ridiculous and out of place among school leavers from the city, who were more confident of themselves. But we knew how not to feel sorry for ourselves, cope with mountains of work and sit in the reading room right until it closed. Within a year many of us country aborigines ranked alongside the best students. Humanitarian interests and knowledge gained from years of reading and a peasant's ambition (we all wanted to be the first in the countryside) helped us to compete with the best in our year and faculty.

For students there were no forbidden themes or topics, even at the turn of the 1950s, when the cult of the leader and the father of the nation reigned. Discussions on cosmopolitanism and patriotism, on the writers Zoshchenko and Akhmatova, the composers Shostakovich and Shaporin, marshals Zhukov and Rokossovsky, the arrival of Alexander Fadeyev, his life in the city and the appearance of the first chapters of his new novel *Ferrous Metallurgy*, the fate of which was as tragic as that of the writer, went on.

The institute was a huge working town of metallurgists and builders. It was a town and factory in one, where everything from the house of culture and theatre to the tramway, stadium and library with the best reading room belonged to the metallurgists. The factory, or works, determined the rhythm of the whole city and influenced the institute as well. We used to frequent the metals works rather than the cinema, seeing for ourselves how the blast and open-hearth furnaces worked and the steel workers in action, night and day. We socialised with many of the young workers, technicians and engineers at evening gatherings and at sporting events. Hardly a month passed in which we did not take part in subbotniks to clear rail tracks of snow, tidy the works up or collect scrap metal. Magnitogorsk, our first and very own city, gave us the fondest memories of our entire lives.

Life's next stage – post-graduate research in Leningrad (now St. Petersburg) – was interesting and full. It lasted all of four years, but its content and influences were varied. They were fortunate years, with time to educate oneself and make up for all the lost learning of those school years. And a fortunate twist of fate lay in the city itself: the opportunity to spend four years in Leningrad and to take advantage of all that unique city, the guardian of Russian traditions, history and culture, had to offer, was a heaven-sent gift. The Leningrad years – 1952-1956, important years in the history of the Fatherland, had a particular meaning for the years to follow. They were a watershed in the nation's conscience, a watershed which has not yet ended.

The years of post-graduate study are happy ones, in which one is able to orientate oneself, one's time, free will and interests. A post-graduate's creative plan is usually divided equally: the first year and a half are spent on examinations and the second on the post-graduate thesis. The essential examinations added little to the former years of study of the history of the Communist Party of the Soviet Union and philosophy. There were simply more source books to read on the subject (at least 200 books of the classics of Marxism-Leninism for each subject), occupying most of the time spent preparing for examinations and leaving almost no time to become familiar with authors not included on the compulsory post-graduate reading list. Afterwards, while working on my thesis, I received special permission to use literature which was banned at the time from the special keeping, and was fortunate enough to read the works of Berdyaev and Kropotkin, the diaries of Nicholas II, the memoirs of Milyukov, Guchkov, Denikin and Krasnov. My supervisor, the phlegmatic and kind-hearted Grigory Pervyshin, studied ancient philosophy but approved my bold efforts (for the times) to write a thesis entitled *Lenin's Teachings on the Revolutionary Situation and Practice of the Great October Revolution.*

At the time, we students of social trends did not imagine that the principal conditions of the revolutionary situation, which required radical changes, 'when the lower classes did not want' to live in the old way and the 'upper classes' could not rule by old methods, had already become deep rooted in Soviet society. The political crises of the 1960s to the 1970s and 1970s to the 1980s led ultimately to the changes that took place in the country in 1985. But there was still a long way to go. Meanwhile Leningrad, with its wealth of Russian cultural history (the Hermitage, Russian Museum, SS Peter and Paul Fortress, Kazan and St. Isaac's cathedrals, the sculpture of Peter the Great outside the Admiralty, symbolising the leanings towards the West), was conducting its own revolution of thought, uniquely broadening our impressions of Fatherland and Russian history.

The post-graduate years (1952-1956) were momentous ones, heralding times of immense change in the country. The first event was the death of Stalin in 1953. Stalin's personality cult had been so great that many could not conceive life in the country without the leader. The second, the Beria case, is now viewed as an ordinary crime connected with the personality cult. However, at the time it opened the black curtain for the first time and all saw what a sordid and bloody dictatorship Stalin's really was. I have never forgotten how we post-graduates, communists from Leningrad, listened to two long evenings of terrifying accusations connected with the Beria case in the University hall. Only then did I understand the secrets shrouded by the blinds of our village district NKVD, secrets which I had tried to work out in my school years.

The next major shock was the 20th Congress of the Communist Party of the Soviet Union in 1956 and Khrushchev's speech dedicated to the Stalin personality cult. The speech was a lightning bolt for the conscience of all who tried to understand what was happening in this country and how we were supposed to live after Stalin. The importance of that Congress lay in that it wiped away the decades of stereotypes engrained in our imagination and opened the floodgates of independent critical thought. Soviet people began to think after long years of mindless obedience.

Those shock waves were so tangible and profound for my own generation that we were never able to forget them. They contained the beginnings of all our subsequent doubts and searchings. Various opinions exist who they, the children of the 20th Congress are. That is a special and broad theme which awaits its chronicler. Suffice it to say here that for all the tremors that the 20th Congress caused, its ideas and evaluations fell on prepared ground.

Life teaches us the following: truth comes sooner or later, and marks its own solemnity and mocks its critics. Only the price of that solemnity is often unbelievably high. All who suffered the tragic consequences of the cult and who had become directly acquainted with the repressions welcomed the 20th Congress as a celebration of justice, if belated. The sixties' generation, from working or peasant families, the offspring of an obliterated intelligentsia, remembered the past and the tragic fate of their fathers and grandfathers. With patience and hope, they waited and prepared for society's revival. Those were people united in their criticism of what had taken place in society. The future of their country was dear to them and they were prepared to bear the responsibility for those serious changes and the hope which the 20th Congress inspired. Perhaps that generation's most important quality was its idealism. Its members were communists, but maintained the older generation's belief in pre-Stalinist socialism, equality, freedom and justice, ideals for which they later paid dearly. They saw that their principles had been trampled into the bloody earth of the repressions and therefore sincerely believed in change, becoming the instruments of that change, no matter what the effort or sacrifice. They stood their ground in the 1970s – the years of stagnation – and themselves formed a human link between the 20th Congress and the perestroika which began in 1985.

The public figures of the years of stagnation are now usually depicted only in dark tones. With that in mind, I often want to ask the critics: 'Where were the ideas of perestroika born, where are their beginnings? Where had those who became the centre of political life after 1985 come from?' Those people were, in fact, the same men and women of the sixties who were unafraid to keep the candle of hope burning in the darkness of apathy and pessimism of the years of stagnation, people who took risks and were bold enough to oppose mediocrity and servility. They were an inspiration, they sowed the seed of popular belief in the inevitability of change.

Leon Trotsky admitted in his book *My Life* that 'national injustice is undoubtedly a major latent stimulus of discontent with the existing order.' For me, that stimulus was the 20th Congress. It helped the sixties' generation wake up fully to their past and become convinced of the unsuitability of the present.

3

My long, 18 years of study were a prelude to life for real, when I would have responsibilities not only for myself. In July 1956, after I had submitted my thesis to Leningrad University, I returned to 'my' Magnitogorsk, but once there, my ambitions received an unexpected slap in the face. Whilst it is true that time heals all injuries, and you begin to realise with the years that misfortunes can also be positive, you must never covet those ambitions too much as there will be no time left for anything else. A city which I had expected to welcome me with open arms welcomed me, in fact, without any warmth. The Mining and Metallurgy Institute, in which I was supposed to have been employed (in the Faculty of Social Sciences), refused to take me on. Only two months later, with pressure from the Gorkom (the city party committee), was I accepted as an assistant with a salary of 105 roubles, and I began to lecture first-years on the history of the Communist Party of the Soviet Union.

Social sciences did not have much authority at this institute, as in many others, where the accent was on training engineers, metallurgists, mining and construction specialists and the like. The Faculty of Social Sciences, which at the time taught the history of the Communist Party, political economy and philosophy, took pains to assert itself at the institute, counting more on the power and authority of the party than on the interest of the students and learning of the lecturers.

From the position of a recent student I was not counting on any outside authority and strove from the beginning to encourage students with the sincerity of my aims. I wanted to draw them into that circle of knowledge which I had amassed over my years of study and instill in them the openness and truth revealed by the 20th Congress of the Communist Party of the Soviet Union. This was 1956, when seminars, a forum for open debate on topics like the personality cult, heroes and the crowd, the leader and the masses, were of great assistance to my quest.

But I must confess that, with hindsight, it is easier to be perspicacious, 35 years on (in 1992), when our criticism of the past is no longer a revelation and Marxism has been exposed and presented as an injurious mistake. It is a far cry from my first steps in the realm of education and sciences as a young lecturer. Looking back and wondering whether I really did withstand the tests of the time, I can say that there is nothing more injurious than the wholesale and peremptory negation, at times assisted by philosophical language, of ideas and teachings. Marxism did stagnate after years of dogmatism. Much became obsolete and our efforts to present it as the only true way for all time brought society nothing but illusion. Marxism as a teaching could not be the only one because it was a natural and organic continuation of the knowledge which society possessed. Notwithstanding, however we may look at Marxism now, it was an unavoidable and important stage in the development of social thought. I am also convinced that the dialectical method of Marxism was and remains one of the most vital instruments of cognition. I saw my role as pedagogue and social scientist then as one who stimulates thought and teaches the listener to make an individual assessment of what goes on in life.

It was then that I found out the true value of scientific activity in the social sciences. The defence of my thesis in Leningrad (which I had to defend again in the Higher Attestation Commission), taught me much. I learned that there was only one author with a monopolist right to propound the dogmas of Marxism-Leninism, and that was the Central Committee of the Communist Party of the Soviet Union. I had distinct impressions of the reasons for the futility of social sciences, the main one being the absence of the most vital ingredients: conflict of opinion, polemics and non-conformism. Without those ingredients, the social sciences become a graveyard, devoid of life.

My daily routine at the institute, the difficult first months becoming accustomed to giving lectures, preparing for seminars, took up most of my time. There was no energy left for anything else. And yet the everyday reality of the working city and demands for involvement penetrated the walls of that institute. The spirit of the times was clearly reflected in work with students at evening classes, which accounted for at least a third of all work at the institute, given the requirements of the metals plant, the renowned Magnitostroi trust and other major enterprises. The evening students brought their everyday problems with them to the institute, comments and attitudes, innovated by the 20th Congress and undisguised by diplomacy.

One of the problems which had to some extent been ignored by public opinion but was now becoming more acute was the ecological situation in Magnitogorsk. The city had been built at immense cost in human terms in a short space of time and had, from the very beginning, been a hostage to the giant metallurgy plant, being built right next to it. Once the first blast and open-hearth furnaces and especially harmful enrichment plants at the foot of Mount Magnitnaya, smelting pig iron, had been launched, hundreds of tonnes of harmful emissions and highly toxic sulphurous gas were spewed out onto the city's inhabitants. Conditions worsened as the plant's capacity was enlarged.

Meanwhile, only after the Second World War did work begin to extend the city on the right bank of the Ural, and then only three to four kilometres away from the metals plant. This all did little to ease conditions for residents, since no measures to limit harmful emission were taken for a long time. I write about this since I too felt the full effect of those harmful emissions, both during my years of study at the Pedagogical Institute (1948-1952) and during other periods of my life and work in the city.

The ecological mess could have been justified in the 1930s and during the war, with the drive to create an industrial potential, the basis of an independent country, and to survive the war years. However, in subsequent years those ecological calamities constantly accompanied industrial expansion in the USSR and brought the nation immense harm. The problem is no less acute today, since a speedy solution is, in many cases, simply impossible. A sobering thought, it is true to say that our ecological problems were caused by our own distorted way of life during the Soviet years.

I have mentioned only one of the city's most burning social issues. There were many more. Residents patiently endured their inconveniences and deprivations for years mainly because they were afraid of speaking out and protesting in the face of an uncompromising administrative regime. Now that the main hurdle, the personality cult, had been removed, people no longer kept their silence. It became obvious that in a society where the slogan '*Everything for Man, All in the Name of Man*' was pronounced, the conditions in which they lived could not be tolerated. The city retained its hundreds of temporary barracks, put up in the 1930s. They did not have rudimentary conveniences, for example lamentable sanitation systems and central heating, and consisted of communal barrack corridors and small rooms (I lived in one myself with my wife's parents during my first year there because the institute did not then provide me with a flat). Roughly a third of the city's population continued to live in those barracks right up to and including the 1960s. The shortage of crèches and kindergartens and school buildings (many schools had to work three shifts), poor medical services (hospitals were also housed in the same barracks next to the metals plant) was also inadmissible. The city, in which over 300,000 people lived and worked, did not have its own hotel, theatre or stadium, and its only two institutions of higher education were in a desperate state.

The problems of the city and country as a whole were the centre of debate at social sciences seminars. They could not be avoided, and had to be answered directly, so that the lecturer could count on the trust of his students. It was then that I and, most likely, many of my colleagues, began to notice serious discrepancies between the real internal party politics, and what we were attempting to present in the face of public opinion. Reality, full of extreme difficulties and conflicts, inevitably exposed contradictions between propaganda and practicality, between word and deed. The awareness of that contradiction could not but give rise to a lack of satisfaction with work as a pedagogue, predominated by old, conventional methods and in which we concealed the truth of life and history behind general declarations on the benefits of socialism and the victorious achievements of our party. On the other hand, the steel workers, who deserved a better life, became aware of those contradictions. They began more and more to raise issues in the very spirit of the 20th Congress. All of this strengthened the belief in the inevitability of change.

Chapter 2 – At Work in the Party

I was training to be a schoolteacher, or perhaps an instructor at one of our institutions of higher education. I saw this as my calling, and devoted many years of study to it. However, Fate has its own ways of dealing with things. In January 1963, at a Party conference, I was elected secretary of the Magnitogorsk city committee. This unexpected event changed a great many of my plans, and became the first great turning point in my life.

The Provincial Party: Its Form and Functioning

How ready and disposed was I towards being a professional Party worker (or, a 'partocrat', as they now say)?

By that time, I was already quite experienced in my chosen profession as a teacher. I had already served nearly eight years at the pedagogical institute. During that time, I had fulfilled all the requirements demanded of me: I had worked as an assistant to a senior instructor, and as a student teacher myself. The last two years, I had headed the department of social sciences. There, of course, I had absolutely no opportunity to acquire any knowledge of the Party's professional canons. However, the reader will perhaps understand me when I say that this turning-point did not seem to me like a cause for great concern.

When you are just over thirty, and it seems that your whole life is in front of you, ambition burns brightly within. You have a desire to prove yourself and see how far you can go; and it seems that your powers and abilities have no limit.

I admit that I was a bit upset, but about something else entirely, something to which I was not accustomed: basically, I now had to start working at something that I had not chosen myself, but directed by those who held positions in the Party. This changes a lot of things for someone who is already used to the perhaps relative, but nevertheless very real, independence of academic life. From that time on, I was a member of the so-called Party nomenklatura, and the CC CPSU (Central Committee of the Communist Party of the Soviet Union), via the regional committee, would now decide my fate.

In contrast to many other institutions and organisations, the Party was rather serious in its selection of members for professional party and government work. The political organisation departments, which essentially handled the cadre work, were the most numerous and influential in the Party committees, and carefully analysed and regulated all the cadre activity. They studied their social composition and the professional qualities of the workers, and actively used adult education courses, party institutes, and the CC CPSU's Academy of Social Sciences to meet these goals. True, there was a great deal of subjectivity in decisions regarding the assignment of cadre personnel; and they were often made by top officials first, and then merely confirmed by the higher Party organs. But this was a well-developed system, and one which had already been functioning for many years.

I think it comes as no great revelation to admit that, in our official guiding principle of democratic centralism, democracy itself was not a major concern. The first secretaries of the district committee, the city committee, and the CPSU's regional committee would gather around themselves their closest colleagues, those who shared their own interests and professional and personal passions. The final word in this, of course, belonged to the Top Man (whoever he might have been); although certainly some corrections could be made, and sometimes were made, by higher Party echelons.

So far as elections to Party committees from below were concerned, I freely admit that their influence was not all that great, as they in practice allowed no alternative candidates. The list of candidates for committee membership was usually worked up in total secrecy by an extraordinarily closed circle of officials, and the rank-and-file Party members could do very little to change the system of alternativeless elections.

Centralism was not the only obstacle to Party democracy. Our professed democracy was also seriously hampered by the strict secretiveness of the Party apparatus's work, starting with the obligatory SECRET stamp on every decision from the district committee on up, and ending with bureau sessions, Party deliberations at every level (which were also regulated), and the selection of Party officials – along with the limited amount of information about them made available to the mass media. I mention this here in order to make the point that it was only from within, by working directly inside the Party apparatus, that one could grasp all the professional peculiarities and the unique content of Party work.

The Magnitogorsk city committee, where I began my Party career, had its own peculiarities which made it different from other city committees subordinate to their regions. Most important of these was that it was a 'factory-city'. The city's basic industrial enterprise was the largest metallurgical combine in the world, which turned out around 14 million metric tonnes of steel a year, along with many millions of tonnes of other various rolled metals. More than 40 thousand people worked at this huge complex. The entire life of the city – its energy supply, living quarters, and public transportation – was totally in the hands of the metallurgical combine. Other large enterprises were also operating in the city: alloy plants, instrument makers, and cement factories, to name a few. However, they could not even be compared with the steel-producing combine, whose influence was all-encompassing. For the Party's city committee, this meant that it had to forego its political authority, and be skilled in maintaining good relations with the heads of the industrial combine.

To further this, in accordance with long-standing tradition, the director of the Magnitogorsk metallurgical combine was a member of the CC CPSU, which placed him higher on the table of Party rank than the CPSU city committee's first secretary. It helped that the director of the combine was a man of great experience, and professional and political authority, who knew how to exercise the tact required to prevent the outbreak of conflict with the Party authorities. At that time, the director of the Magnitogorsk metallurgical combine was Feodosi Voronov, a man well known among this country's metallurgists, and a respected specialist in the area of steel smelting. He was a member of the CC CPSU, a deputy of the Supreme Soviet of the RSFSR (Russian Soviet Federalist Socialist Republic), and later worked in Moscow as a first deputy to the Minister of Ferrous Metallurgy of the USSR. Working together with him was not without its problems, but an understanding did exist. The industrial leader considered second in importance in the city was the director of the Magnitostroi building trust. This was the same trust that had built both the metallurgical complex, and the city of Magnitogorsk itself. During the war years, Magnitostroi was headed by the famous (in this country) industrial expert Veniamin Dymshits, who later became a deputy to the Chairman of the Council of Ministers of the USSR. The director of the Magnitostroi trust at this time was Leonid Ankudinov, a man who had risen from one of Magnitogorsk's ground-breaking construction workers, all the way to first director of the trust. He was a man of few words, but caring and generous in his deeds.

Obviously, the time has still not come where it is possible to dispassionately judge just who these provincial Party workers really were. Time has brought about a great many changes in the appearance, way of life, and activities of these 'partocrats', who are today called responsible for all our country's woes. One had to go through the Magnitogorsk professional school in order to grasp, basing on one's own personal experience, what was characteristic of our society as a whole: that the Party was the basic mechanism of an administrative system that directed all spheres of life in an enormous country.

For me, someone who had gone straight from an institute into Party work, the question of just what was the Party became first of all a question of hands-on working experience. The city's entire economic sphere was in practice directly controlled by Party authorities; while the Soviets were relegated to a beggar's role, and were roundly criticised from all sides. This evoked many questions which were difficult to answer. In Magnitogorsk, which was a living example of all that had been born during the years of Soviet power, there were a number of especially noticeable contradictions between the interests of production and those of the human beings there. In all its declarations, the Party emphasised that the most important thing in all its actions was mankind, and its concern for it. In real life, it so happened that mankind, with its interests and needs, took a distant back seat to the Plan.

I have already spoken about the serious problem of air pollution and all the dirt fouling the city of Magnitogorsk. This led to major conflicts as the combine's power grew greater, and it was completely useless to even speak of a general cleaning-up. The energies of the Party's city council were entirely directed to the further development of the metallurgical combine: the construction of new smelting ovens and rolling mills. At the same time, Magnitogorsk embarked on the construction of the country's largest mills for the rolling of tin, and wide-strip sheets for the production of automobile bodies. Construction was completed on the ninth of the country's largest blast furnaces, with an annual production of more than a million tonnes of pig iron, and work on the tenth began immediately afterwards. Party workers sat for months at these huge construction sites, playing the roles of head administrators and materials suppliers. It was with less difficulty that the city committee and its staff provided decisions on all other questions of production, where the number one concern was the fulfilment of the plans to supply metal to hundreds of locations. Dozens of telegrams came in daily from all corners of the country, and staff members from the industrial division actively worked with them to cut through all the red tape involved.

The Party's city committee, performing the role of main administrative-distribution organ, viewed ideological activity only as an aid in fulfilling its production goals, although its inability to solve many serious questions of housing, education, and recreation for the workers was obvious from all the great and irreparable losses we sustained, and the inattention it paid towards the average person. It was with great pain that I thought and, in my speeches to the CPSU regional committee, openly spoke about the disproportionate means being spent on the development of production, and the social needs of the city's inhabitants. The enterprises of Magnitogorsk brought the country tens of millions of roubles in profits. The city's production, in the monetary terms of those days, can be expressed as more than 2 billion roubles; and the amount spent on meeting the needs of housing, medical care, and public education was, in comparison to our profits, a paltry sum.

Of all the institutions in the city, the establishments of culture and the arts were by far the poorest, and without the support of the various enterprises could not have survived. A lot was kept going in the city thanks only to the enthusiasm of certain champions of culture, people who were unselfish and giving. The city's drama theatre was especially popular; it was headed by the Honoured Artist of the RSFSR Anatoli Rezinin, a man totally devoted to his work as chief director.

The State Choir, headed by People's Artist of the RSFSR Semyon Eidinov, was also much beloved by the city's inhabitants. The Choir was, in large measure due to its highly gifted director, Eidinov, among the most famous professional choral collectives in the country. Eidinov was also known in the city as a man who gave all his time to musical enlightenment for the masses. Actors, musicians, workers at Houses of Culture, clubs, libraries – they brought so much that was good and bright to the lives of people, and asked for so little in return.

The real generator of cultural life in the city was Natalya Platonova, the head of the cultural section of the city committee's executive board. She was a person of rare spirit, one who was outstanding in her surprising selflessness and kindness. My long-standing friendship with her, from then all the way down to today, helps me and my family to keep our faith in the goodness of people through the most difficult of times.

I remember from that long-ago time just how often the Party workers had to work long and hard, and use all their patience and tact, to convince the economic managers that man does not live by bread alone. For all our efforts, the returns were not great; just as the current authorities' neglect of the arts is by no means something new.

Particularly memorable during these years was the holding, in the spring of 1966, of the first all-Union meeting of the original builders of Magnitogorsk. This was a wonderful get-together with those who, during the trying 1930s, created the metallurgical complex and city of Magnitogorsk on the steppes of the South Urals. A monument to the original builders was raised for the occasion: a concrete tent, the creation of the famous Urals sculptor Lev Golovnitsky, was erected on the right bank of the Ural River. A park to the original builders of Magnitogorsk has since grown up around the site.

Among the veterans attending was Boris Ruchyov, Magnitogorsk's fine poet, and a man with a difficult and tragic fate: having experienced for years the tortures of the GULAG, he had returned to Magnitogorsk only after 1953. Ruchyov attained great fame all over the country for his wonderful poetic talents. To this day, I can hear his scratchy voice, which sounded as though he had caught a permanent cold in a Siberian forest, reciting the lines:

> *We lived in a tent with a little green window;*
> *That was washed by the rain, and dried by the sun;*
> *And golden campfires burned at our doors;*
> *On the rust-coloured rocks of Magnet Mountain.*

In reminiscing about Boris Ruchyov, I cannot help but make one small digression. In one of our conversations, I asked him about the ill feeling I thought he should have towards the older generation, whose fault it was that he – a young member of the writers' union in the 1930s, one who had been recommended by Maxim Gorky himself, and one who had participated in the first congress of writers of the USSR – had been thrown into a GULAG concentration camp on the basis of nothing but somebody's evil scheming. He was silent a while, and then said: 'I can see by your question that you're still young, and that you still have no appreciation of the problems of the past. But I think that you can't judge those who go before you, since you always have to remember that there are also those who are coming after you.'

It is well known that the only condition evil needs to exist is that good people remain silent, and endure the cruelty that happens in life. Now, when so much is being done to break the ties between generations and to harden people to the past, I think about Magnitogorsk and the older generation. Of what can this generation be guilty before the current young masters of life? Of the fact that they, hungry and freezing in their ice-cold barracks during the harsh 1930s, built this giant metallurgical complex and enormous city, where there now live more than 400,000 people. They sincerely believed that they were building not simply a city, but creating a steel heart for the Motherland, to whose work rhythm this entire huge country would live. Whether or not we would remain a country depended greatly on how that steel heart beat during the deadly years of the Great Patriotic War [World War II - *tr*.]. The older generation lived hard and knew little of the comforts that we know today. They got little of what they deserved, but they knew how to work like no one else. No, I don't believe that the ties of time will be broken, and the young people will cease to respect and revere those who travelled down the difficult road before them.

Four years have gone by since I had to change my profession and entire way of life. This time has been filled to the limit with conferences, meetings, and get-togethers with different people. Being in the thick of things happening in the city, and the many different concerns I had to deal with daily for ten to twelve hours at a time, gave me a lot of food for thought in understanding the problems that people lived with. I will admit that the work of a city committee secretary, loaded to the limit with a multitude of daily concerns, is not conducive to taking one's time to mull over and analyse the complicated processes taking place in the country, since we were counted on to carry out orders that came from above. At the same time, this was the stormy period of reform under Nikita Khrushchev. It was a time of noisy, well-publicised interregional conferences on the problems of agriculture, during which Khrushchev critically examined regional leaders on their knowledge of agricultural problems. The first to fall victims to such exams in Sverdlovsk were the leaders of the Chelyabinsk Region – N.V. Laptev and V.V. Rusak, the first and second secretaries of the regional committee, and A.A. Bezdomov, chairman of the regional executive committee.

This period is famous for the conducting of experiments which were most original in form, and most awkward in their execution – the division of Party committees in every administrative region into city/industrial and rural/agrarian. The clumsiness of such a division was obvious since, on the one hand, the Party's transformation into the economic-administrative structure grew even stronger; and on the other, the split between the city and the countryside, which was ruinous for our already lagging agricultural production, also grew much greater. I will repeat, however, that provincial party workers never had to think, and we were certainly never taught to seriously ponder what was going on in the Party or the rest of the country. It was with singular zeal, therefore, that rural district committees in the villages were first created, and then dissolved, by order of the CC CPSU, which customarily argued its position with references to one or another of Lenin's theses and citations. This also happened with various committees for Party and government control, as well as with *sovnarkhozi*, or national economics ministries.

I admit that the Party's decision to relieve Khrushchev of his duties in the autumn of 1966 was made just as calmly and blandly. This happened not only because mindless obedience prevailed in the Party, but also because the endless reforms and changes evoked uneasiness and insecurity in the Party committees. Meanwhile, because of this, neither the national economy nor the lives of the Soviet people were getting any better, and the 'chicken in every pot' that Khrushchev had promised the people had to be delayed. No one particularly wished Khrushchev any ill, but people stopped believing in him. As a result, his dismissal was not seen as a conspiracy or *coup d'état*, but was met with as the natural exit of a man whose potential as supreme leader was exhausted.

The changes at the centre of the Party had an unexpected influence on my destiny. In October 1967, I was confirmed as director of the CPSU regional committee's department of science and educational institutions, and moved to Chelyabinsk.

I admit that, no matter how difficult work was in the city committee, I was more independent in my actions there, and I didn't really want to leave it; mostly, however, it was hard to leave the city to which I was indebted for so much. There was nothing else I could do, though: Party discipline bound me to obedience.

My moving to Chelyabinsk, as it later became known, was connected with the earlier departure for Moscow of Y.M. Tyazhelnikov, who was at that time working as secretary to the Party's Chelyabinsk regional committee. It happened that his position in the CPSU regional committee came down to me in June 1967. Work in Chelyabinsk, in the CPSU regional committee, had its advantages. To a large degree, I associate this with the arrival as leader of the Chelyabinsk Party organisation of Nikolai Rodionov, a man who had great intellectual and professional potential. Before Chelyabinsk, Rodionov was well known as the first secretary of the Leningrad city committee, and as the second secretary of the Kazakhstan CC during the conquest of the Virgin Lands. Not having gotten along with the local leaders in Kazakhstan, he returned to the *sovnakhoz* (people's economy council) in Leningrad. As fortune would have it, he was recommended to go to Chelyabinsk as the first secretary of the regional Party committee in 1966.

The Chelyabinsk Region differed from others above all in its huge volume of industrial production, and was ranked in the top ten greatest industrial areas in the country. Besides Magnitogorsk, such cities as Zlatoust, Kopeisk, and Miass were well known across the country, as well as a number of closed (but known to all) cities specialising in the production of awesome nuclear weapons. As a result of this, the region's inhabitants were the first to experience the frightening, Chernobyl-like consequences of nuclear disasters in the 1950s. Also well known were certain giant industrial enterprises: the Chelyabinsk tractor factory, the Chelyabinsk and Zlatoust metallurgical plants, the Chelyabinsk pipe-rolling and Miass automobile factories, and dozens of others. The region was also different by virtue of its remarkable feats, especially during the war years, when Chelyabinsk became one of our main weapons producers, and was famous the world over as 'Tankograd'.

The inhabitants of Chelyabinsk left fond memories of themselves among their compatriots in that during the darkest days of the war, and of the reconstruction period that followed, they did a great deal to create a vast industrial potential in the region. This potential, at the cost of many unrewarded sacrifices by ordinary people, served the country and helped it to stand firm and win in that crucial period when the industry of the western regions had been lost. The principle of my generation, think of the Motherland first, and then of yourself – which was well known in the past, but is currently maligned by zealous muck-rakers – was perhaps most taken to heart by those who lived and worked in the Chelyabinsk region, where it determined their character and way of life. The workers of the region and its leaders were different in their traditional modesty and simplicity, and their inability to defend their own interests when faced by Moscow. This was in contrast to their northern neighbours, the Sverdlovskites, and is, I think, the main reason why it is so hard for them today to defend their independence and solve the many difficult social problems that remain from the past.

The current destructive influences so well known to all were born with the adoption of the idea of sovereignisation, which was proclaimed in June 1990 by Russia's First Congress of People's Deputies, and became irreversible with its violation of a single Russian state. Quite a bit has already been said and written about this. However, much less has been said about the reasons for (and sources of) this idea. Meanwhile, to be objective about it, one must recognise that there were some extremely serious grounds for the formation of the idea of Russian sovereignty, connected with the decades-long absence of rights of the RSFSR within the single family of Union republics.

They can probably accuse me of having a Russian great-power complex, but I must say exactly what my convictions are. Everyone knows that the industrial and intellectual potential of the Union republics was, for many years, created largely at the expense of Russia, and the depletion and impoverishment of her native territories – the depopulated and drained Black Earth Zone is a convincing example of this. I'm not talking about this second-hand, or without bitterness, since over a period of eight years, the future editor-in-chief of the newspaper *Sovetskaya Rossiya* was present almost daily at the meetings of the Council of Ministers of the RSFSR. He was a witness to these open displays of lawlessness, and the resulting uselessness of the Russian leadership, regardless of who headed it – Voronov or Solomentsev, Vorotnikov or Vlasov.

As a result of my origins, I have been asked many times: 'How is the provincial Party different from the centre Party?'

I will answer this question honestly, without trying to hide my own personal bias. Compared to the Centre, the provinces are much more open and direct in their day-to-day relations, and there is less hypocrisy and more trust between people. However, I am not ready to idealise the provinces, since this would mean closing my eyes to their numerous defects. Among these are the well-known traditional subservience and deference to the Centre, and a striving to curry its favour with industriousness and discipline. In their zeal to copy the Centre in everything, the provinces display a marked obsequiousness, which was tortuous for any person inclined to having their own opinions. Let us recall the wisdom of the Russian classics: 'To serve is a joy; to be a servant is nauseating.'

The obsequiousness in the provinces was at once tortuous and all-mighty, since everything most often depended on the aristocratic haughtiness of the first Party officer. This haughtiness depended least of all on the merit of the individual, since it was simply an essential attribute of Party power.

I know from personal experience that skilled associates were always found who very quickly created around the first secretary an aura of superiority, special privileges and rights, and created for these purposes a definite ritual of conduct – one which was strictly upheld by the leader himself, and whose observance became absolutely mandatory: the first secretary always came first, seated himself at meetings first, had car number 00-01 (the number two man had 00-02), etc. I remember that I often had a strong desire to make the awkwardness of this established ritual even greater, and introduce numbers of precedence for the backs of the secretaries and members of the regional committee bureau, rather like on the uniforms of hockey players, so that no one would confuse just who occupied which place in the table of ranks, and thereby fail to render the obligatory honours.

Whether it was due to a sudden change in age (I turned 40 in Chelyabinsk), or whether it was due to my nature, and the genes I inherited, I grew more and more dejected by this provincial Party pretence and obsequiousness, which evoked not only feelings of disgust and irritation, but also unbearable offence at my own self-denigration. At these moments, I always felt ashamed of myself. More and more often, I felt helpless and all alone in my longing to fight against this stifling atmosphere of obedience. At this time too, I would recall the writings of Yevgeni Yevtushenko:

> *The forties are a funny time,*
> *When you're still young, but not young,*
> *And oldsters cannot understand you,*
> *And youth, you understand, is not so wise.*

You don't need a voice to sing in a choir of obsequiousness; you just have to know when to open your mouth along with everyone else. Unfortunately (or perhaps, fortunately) God did not grant me this skill, and on account of this, apparently, all the turning points in my life were sharp ones.

Meanwhile, my time living in Chelyabinsk was coming to an end. I won't hide the fact that I felt this was coming in talks which were held between me and P.N. Demichev, who was at that time the secretary of the CC CPSU in charge of questions of ideological work; and in conversations in the CC propaganda department, with the department deputy directors A.N. Yakovlev and G.L. Smirnov. Talk at these meetings was of the advisability of my transferring to work on the staff of the CC CPSU propaganda department. Before, in 1973, I had explained my refusal to do so on account of the short time since my arrival in the Chelyabinsk regional committee, and the need to allow me the opportunity of working a bit in the district. However, these discussions were continued in 1975, after Yakovlev was no longer a member of the propaganda department, and Demichev had been transferred from the CC and appointed Minister of Culture of the USSR. It was much harder to explain my further refusal.

The situation in the Chelyabinsk regional committee had changed too, as in 1973 N.N. Rodionov was transferred to work in the USSR Ministry of Foreign Affairs, as a deputy minister. This had an immediate effect on the entire atmosphere of the CPSU Chelyabinsk regional committee. The work became uninteresting, and my striving for independence was more and more viewed unfavourably.

And when, in August 1975, I was once again invited to join the CC CPSU, I passed into the highest echelons of Party power: I first spoke with I.V. Kapitonov, then with A.P. Kirilenko, and finally with M.A. Suslov. By this time, I had no further decision to make, other than to agree to come to Moscow and start work at the CC CPSU department of propaganda, as a deputy department director. Thus began my service at the Party's centre, which brought me so much woe, and so little joy.

The Party Centre: Staraya Square and Its Inhabitants

Things are difficult and uncomfortable for a provincial in the capital, especially at first. Everything around you seems strange and unusual. It becomes clear that to move at a mature age to a city completely unknown to you (especially if that city happens to be Moscow) is not only not easy; one risks the loss of one's self.

I will allow myself to make a digression and describe the impressions that Moscow life made on me at the very beginning. In order to live in Moscow without feeling like you're an outsider, one must be born there. A newcomer to the capital meets with numerous instances of insincerity, hypocrisy, clannishness, and prejudices. In contrast to what is accepted behaviour in the Urals, Moscow frowns on directness in relationships, preferring that people hide their feelings, and openness is considered a sign of an undesirable tone. I think that it is no accident that 'Moscow does not believe in tears', since suffering and showing sympathy are held in such low esteem. Now too on account of this, when it is such a difficult time for the country as a whole, it is especially difficult for someone in Moscow to resist being humiliated and maintain their dignity. It is sad to see that the relationships existing in Moscow are beginning to have a very rapid effect on the people who ended up in Moscow earlier, and rather quickly mastered the customs of capital life. This has happened because, being used to obedience, it is difficult for the provincial to maintain his independence. My grandfather, a Cossack sergeant, spoke about this quite often: 'It's a bad thing to be dumb, and never have to develop a strong mind.'

Perhaps I too am a bit biased in my dislike for the capital; I hope, however, that any observant person will agree with me that, just as relations between people are perverted in Moscow, so too does a certain rudeness prevail among them. Whenever acquaintances meet, they make the traditional exclamation: We have to get together and spend some time with each other. This ritual always finishes with both sides shouting the promise: I'll call you. But weeks go by, then months, and no one calls, and no one arranges to get together. And you, in your provincial ignorance, remain alone with your worries and confusion; and gradually, you get used to the fact that help and sympathy wait for you nowhere in the capital, and that you have to rely only on yourself.

Back then, this witty, well-known definition often came to mind: 'A simpleton is somebody who, in response to the strictly formal question whenever acquaintances meet, "Hey! How're you doin'?", seriously launches into a detailed explanation of how he's doing.' This is how much a simpleton I looked my first few months in Moscow, taking into account my provincial directness, and cursing the day that I decided to move to Moscow.

Formalism and window-dressing appear everywhere in the capital, in ways large and small. I remember 6 November 1975, our first anniversary of the Bolshevik Revolution in Moscow, my wife and I met, at a ceremonial session of the Palace of Congresses, two other provincials who were just as nervous as we were – Nikolai Ryzhkov and his wife, Ludmila. They too had just arrived in Moscow, where Nikolai had begun work as a deputy minister for heavy industry. Having been acquaintances in the Urals, we greeted each other like long-lost relatives, since it was obvious to anyone watching that they, like us, felt lonely and estranged in the world of the capital. I noticed then, and realised later, that most often it was also only provincials who went to ceremonial sessions with their wives.

Getting established in the apparatus of the CC CPSU, in contrast to the Chelyabinsk regional committee, was pure hell.

Thinking about this 16 years later, I can see that this was connected not simply with another style of work, but also with completely different rules of mutual relationships, and other strict demands of subordination at all levels of duty, from instructors all the way up to the secretary of the CC. Staraya Square and its inhabitants lived according to their own laws and customs, known only to them and followed impeccably.

The mechanism of the apparatus had been created over the many years of the Party's monopoly position in directing all spheres of life in society, and functioned on the basis of harsh discipline and immediate, almost unquestioning, obedience. In the CC apparatus, it was not acceptable to delegate one's personal responsibilities in any way to one or another fellow worker; everyone was just a small part, the notorious 'cog' in a big machine, the results of whose work were impersonal and considered to be collective. The right to be named, or to authorship, belonged primarily only to the secretaries of the CC, although the reports they gave, and the articles published under their name in the press, were always the result of work by the apparatus's large collective of rank-and-file workers.

I must admit that working in the apparatus of the CC CPSU was a good school for taming my vanity, and learning the principles of organisation and discipline, which allowed me to master analysing the processes that were under way in the country. However, the cost of this was high, since, on the other hand, it stripped the worker of any kind of independence, and weaned him away from initiative. In the CC apparatus, obedience and devotion to duty were valued above all. Any attempts to somehow express one's private opinion, or make one's position known in speeches to an audience or in the press, met first with disapproval, were then accompanied by open criticism, and could end with dismissal from one's post. In my own experience, I managed to expose myself to all these different attitudes towards those who thought differently.

There was only an extremely small group of apparatus workers (apparatchniks) who belonged to the élite: these were the assistants to the General Secretary, and the assistants to the secretaries and members of the Politburo Mikhail Suslov and Andrei Kirilenko, who had practically unlimited rights to the intellectual exploitation of any of the department's workers, and to the use of the creative property of any instructor, consultant, sector chief, chairman, or department head. There are good grounds for calling the period of Leonid Brezhnev's Party rule, especially the last few years, the era of the apparatus assistants' omnipotence. I think that this was unavoidable, since the more inert and helpless the Chief became mentally and physically, the more zealous and daring his servants became, especially those in the circle closest to the top man.

Just a short time after my arrival in the CC apparatus, it had already become clear that the place of every worker there had been determined in advance, and forever. It was only within the limits of the space allotted him that a worker could move, turn around, have an opinion, and introduce proposals, without stepping over the established boundaries. The hierarchy of Party power, subordination, and dependency was also firmly established, and had been unshakable for many years. Only the most extraordinary circumstances or events, having become the property of a large segment of public opinion, could have brought about change in that indestructible order.

I will mention just one example of this. Usually, the activities of the CC CPSU secretaries and members of the Politburo, with the help of their nearest associates, were deliberately shrouded in an impenetrable veil of secrecy and security, with an obligatory emphasis on the top plan of the especially significant and influential person of the highly-placed Party leader. And only unforeseen events would suddenly make obvious to all that, behind the veil, there was sometimes simply nothing – the emperor had no clothes!

The grandiose confusion that took place with Andrei Kirilenko, during the period when he was aspiring to the role of number two man in the Party, and even trying to somehow destroy Mikhail Suslov's omnipotence in the CC CPSU, is remembered by many. The uproar happened at the 26th Congress of the CPSU, during the final days of its work, when, in order to distinguish the leaders of the Party and simultaneously raise the importance of the proposed members and candidate members of the CC CPSU, it was decided that Suslov would read the list of those proposed members to be voted upon, and the list of the candidate members would be read by Kirilenko. Suslov's reading of his list went without any particular difficulties. But when Kirilenko began reading his list of proposed candidate members from the lectern, it became obvious to the delegates assembled that before them was a man who either didn't know how to read, or who was in the final stages of mental and physical deterioration. All those present at the congress could not hide a certain feeling of shame when he couldn't correctly pronounce, or read all the way through, a single one of the names on the list, which contained just a little over 100 people. Assumptions of Kirilenko's long-standing and deep sclerosis had become reality. And this man, in this condition, having been at the heights of Party power, had enjoyed the highest right to 'sentence and pardon'. It was only after this that he was eventually, and with great difficulty, driven into retirement.

Working for weeks and months at Party country homes, on the preparation of reports for international deliberations, CC plenums, and general meetings was, as is any kind of impersonal work, unproductive and inefficient, and unimportant in the creative sense. Often, two or three groups worked in parallel on the same material for a report, and yet a fourth would put the finishing touches on it. The result of this was that everything prepared by the groups in the initial stage often turned out to be unacceptable, especially if the authors proposed any new ideas or unorthodox approaches.

Such an unproductive approach in the organisation of work unavoidably led to the fact that the majority of workers in the CC CPSU apparatus were primarily occupied with the preparation of various papers. All the department workers were continually writing something.

The opportunity and right to directly analyse the processes at work in daily life in the republics, regions, and districts belonged only to certain individual workers. There were very few of these, most often only from the departments for Party organisational work, and their branch offices. Even in this instance, there were extremely few of these who were not busy with the preparation for publication of directories, project decisions, reports, and speeches. Those who, for one reason or another, got used to the well-regulated mechanism of apparatus work, finally learnt: Don't assume responsibility for the final result, don't display any special zeal, and don't take on too much work; take on just the right amount so that you can accomplish only that to which you've been assigned. Don't stand out – this may sound crude, but they knew what they were talking about back then in the CC CPSU apparatus, when they advised you to live with minimal losses and expenditure of nervous energy, and without overly taxing your intellect.

After the regional committee, where I, in the role of secretary, had within the boundaries of my functioning a certain – albeit limited – independence and right to initiative (even if it was not always upheld), within the apparatus of the CC CPSU I immediately found myself inside a rigid framework, which was strictly required for the observance of norms and the rules of conduct. My first impression of work in the apparatus was literally that I had been dressed in a new suit and made to wear new shoes, but that everything had been made a size too small; and you always feel as though everything is too tight, and it's uncomfortable for you to walk, sit, and think.

The difficulties in getting established were made even worse by the fact that, in the role of deputy director of the propaganda department, I was expected to master a sphere of activity completely new to me – international information. My duties included coordinating the activities of such central ideological establishments as TASS, the Novosti press agency, and VAAP (USSR Copyright Agency). I was also responsible for coming up with proposals for the development of ideological cooperation with the communist parties of other socialist countries, and much else.

The content of this work involved the propaganda department's relations with international departments, and therefore much depended on my contacts and connections with colleagues working in related areas.

In Chelyabinsk, the sphere of my activities had no such international aspects, and it was therefore difficult, especially at first, to become a useful partner of such experienced and highly-qualified international department staff as V.V. Zagladin, A.S. Chernyayev, G.Kh. Shakhnazarov, *et al.* Against all expectations, and in spite of own fears, within 3-4 months I had already managed to make working contacts with my more experienced colleagues, and then work together with them meaningfully during my years in the CC, all the while maintaining good, friendly relations with them. To the characteristics of my colleagues from the international departments, I will add only that their experience – which, I freely admit, I (as a provincial newcomer) had originally envied – was to a large degree expressed in the fact that they knew very well what their higher leadership needed from them, and handed up only that which they wanted to receive, and not one iota more.

Such an approach was natural for them, since it flowed logically from that peculiarity of the apparatus mechanism, whereby you did not simply fulfil one or another function of your duties on your own, but worked significantly more on assignments handed down by your superiors, in which your individuality and personal input was of no interest to anyone. Therefore, along with experience, an apparatus worker very quickly tried most of all to understand what was of interest to his immediate superior; or for what his group had been formed, and the material was being prepared. In this 'art of obedience', and the meeting of the corresponding needs of their suzerain, experienced apparatus workers had reached a hitherto unseen perfection. I was always struck by the skill of the international department's workers whenever I read a prepared report, and then listened to the speeches of B.N. Ponomarev (their boss) at international conferences. The CC CPSU international department's consultants, under the leadership of A.S. Chernyayev, always prepared for their boss a report in which were observed not only all the peculiarities, but even the intonations of Ponomarev's speech, taking into account his manner of delivery, and the tone of the address. To write such an address, in which the CC secretary didn't even put a comma, a Party worker had to acquire the highest kind of skill in the apparatus arts.

I will come back to this, however, to continue the story about working conditions in the CC propaganda department of that period. They were unusual, to say the least. The fact of the matter was, that after the famous uproar that occurred with the theses of the CC CPSU, prepared by the propaganda department's workers for the 100th anniversary of Lenin's birth (and which, for the sake of revisionism, contained citations that were in no way attributable to him), there unfolded a major scandal which had quite large international repercussions. This uproar, incidentally, is a good example of the mindless, impersonal executive style that had been mastered by the CC CPSU. As a result, the head of the propaganda department – the irreplaceable V.I. Stepakov, who, for a short time following the release of Nikita Khrushchev served as the secretary of the Moscow regional committee of the CPSU, the editor-in-chief of the newspaper *Izvestia*, and as department head for the CC CPSU – was released from his duties, and made ambassador to Yugoslavia. I won't judge him too harshly here, since he was only carrying out that which had been assigned to him: He had been assigned the task of calming the ideological passions that had arisen during the early Khrushchev era, and fitting everything back in the old mould of dogmatic political thought. He was kept well informed as to what Lenin (and his opponents) had said, but only to the degree of the propaganda department workers' erudition – which, as it turned out, was not terribly great.

A short time after this, in connection with a well-known address in *Literaturnaya gazeta*, A.N. Yakovlev was released from his duties as deputy department head, for 'excessive zealousness'. Soon thereafter, CC CPSU secretary P.N. Demichev, who got along with everyone, was transferred to the Ministry of Culture.

All sessions of the Secretariat, during my tenure, were chaired by Mikhail Suslov, and during his rare absences only, Andrei Kirilenko. The Secretariat ruled the departments strictly and unconditionally. Many of its decisions were prepared and remained the common property of the narrow circle of people who took part in their preparation. It often happened that a decision by the CC CPSU

Secretariat would appear which mainly evaluated the work of some central ideological establishment, and even contained some serious conclusions; but the department's workers were usually kept in total ignorance, and were usually assigned only the execution of the task.

This would happen because a large number of the decisions were prepared by a narrow circle of people, and adopted without discussion only by the individual votes of the secretaries. I remember, in June 1976, without the slightest participation of the propaganda department, the CC CPSU Secretariat's decision *On the Work of the Novosti Press Agency* was adopted, in which its work was evaluated extremely negatively; as a result, the department chairman, I.I. Udaltsov, and his first deputy, A.I. Vlasov, were released from their duties. Simultaneously, the information and television services were dissolved, and a significant reduction in the apparatus was made – more than 50 of the most qualified workers were let go from the agency, according to a special list; to this day, no one knows who drew it up. I remember how difficult it was to hide my bewilderment when this list was handed to me personally by M.V. Zimyanin, who had just become a secretary of the CC. To my naive question, 'Where did this list come from?' Zimyanin answered that he was not authorised to give me that information, and I think that this was the case. He was, however, authorised to tell me that my assignment was to invite all those who appeared on the blacklist (I guessed that it had been compiled by the KGB), and let them know that they'd been fired for essentially no reason at all. I remember what internal torture I experienced during these talks, trying not to offend these (as I felt) innocent people, and helping them as much as it was within my power to transfer to some other kind of work. I was pleased when, after these not very happy meetings, I was able to maintain good relations with many of them – A. Vlasov, V. Nekrasov, V. Shevchenko, V. Katin, to name a few.

What am I leading up to here? To an attempt to answer the question: Just who was running the Party? Lev Onikov, a former Party functionary, in answering this question in one of the April 1992 editions of the newspaper *Pravda*, confided a number of observations on this point. In doing so, he divides the entire internal structure of the Party into four basic parts. The first is the rank-

and-file Party members, its most numerous part – 18.7 million people. The second part is the members of the leading (elected) organs, from the district committees right up to the CCs of the republic communist parties – 439 thousand people. The third part is the secretaries of the Party committees, from the regional committees up to the republic CCs, excluding the CC CPSU apparatus – 86 thousand people.

The fourth part consists of the highest echelons of the Party – the members and candidate members of the CC CPSU (elected at the 27th Congress), 477 people; the members and candidate members of the Politburo, and secretaries of the CC CPSU, 32 people; and the CC CPSU apparatus staff, 1383 people. Onikov concludes that the 99.7% of the Party's members were totally without power, and only the 0.3% belonging to the higher echelons – the members and candidate members of the CC and Politburo, and the members of the Secretariat, actually had power. However, all the Party's affairs were decided upon, in his opinion, by only the members of the Politburo and Secretariat – the same 32 people who belonged to the ruling Party élite.

There is a great deal that is just in Onikov's assessment, although it simplifies the process of governing by such a complex, giant body as the Party was itself, since it does not take at all into account the diffusion of Party power, and the peculiarities of its manifestation in all the Party's structural divisions, beginning at the most elementary Party organisation. The Party, if one tries to visualise it, was a giant ship-of-the-line, the motion of which was controlled by hundreds of hands, standing at various mechanisms, without which movement would have been impossible – although at the helm stood only one person. In order to objectively evaluate the Party's system of rule, one must know very well the character of the relationships between all of its units and the centre, and know who was in charge of and responsible for the regional, city, district, factory, and state farm Party committees. Without having any influence upon Party policy, the CPSU regional committees had full powers to settle social and economic questions on the local level.

I can, however, agree fully that the Party's internal and external policies were in fact determined by the 32 men at the highest echelons of power, and the influence of the provincial Party in this really was practically nil.

I will say, however, that after the 27th Congress of the CPSU too, there was an enormous opportunity to influence the state of affairs in the Party. It was only the old inertia of obedience, and the lack of true leaders in the regions that prevented this. But this is getting ahead of myself.

The content and style of the Secretariat's work at that time was determined from beginning to end by Mikhail Suslov. A large portion of the secretaries present – or even more so, the department workers invited to attend sessions of the Secretariat – usually were extras, playing the role of an attentive supporting cast; objections to anything were the rare exception. Meanwhile, I wouldn't begin to describe Suslov only as a person of limited mentality, or someone on the wane, playing the part of the Grey Cardinal. I mention this since I don't agree with a lot of what has been written on the topic. I admit that, in evaluating the recent past, I don't really care to present myself in the role of an all-seeing, all-knowing character like Fyodor Burlatsky, and paint all the people who managed to make it back then as thick retrogrades, ignorant and limited in thought. I don't agree with that kind of approach, since the truth suffers as a result of elevating yourself, and the times in which you live. Even in the appellation 'the Grey Cardinal', I always see more tribute to historical parallels than to actual fact. With regard to the CC, Suslov was not a 'Grey Cardinal', as he ruled the CC CPSU apparatus with virtually unlimited power, and yet without making himself prominent. In essence, he was a living embodiment of Party conservatism, from his old-fashioned clothes and his famous galoshes, to the principles which he professed: Don't think, don't invent anything; just do everything the way it's always been done. In his work, Mikhail Suslov, with the utmost devotion and diligence, reflected the Party policies of the Brezhnev era, the essence of which was to steadfastly maintain the existing order of things.

Along with this, I will say that Suslov was a real character. He was one of those who really believed in the communist idea; the only other Party leader of that time whom I would call as faithful was Yuri Andropov. He was completely without pretence: he always remained the epitome of the highly-organised person, and a pedant with the manner of a teacher at a Tsarist-era gymnasium. Always precise, always laconic, he never engaged in idle chatter while chairing meetings of the Secretariat. Only an extraordinary event would be a reason for a meeting to last more than an hour, or a speech more than 5-7 minutes. Any longer, and Suslov would automatically say 'Thank you', and the embarrassed speaker would gather up his papers. I admit that myself and newspaper editors V. Afanasyev and L. Tolkunov, having been participants at those sessions, often thought of Suslov when his spot as chairman of the CC Secretariat was occupied by first Chernenko, and then Gorbachev: unrestrained and hours-long debates engulfed sessions of the Party's executive organ like waves of muddy water.

One must, however, admit that the precisely organised work of the Secretariat was not notable for its basic creative approach. It was simply impossible to make it public, since everything went from year to year according to a strictly enforced order and was subject only to precedent. They would report, for example, from the Academy of Sciences that 'in San Francisco, the 7th International Congress of Oceanographers will soon take place. We request your permission for a group of scholars from the USSR to attend.' And Suslov would invariably ask, 'And how many Soviet scholars were there at the previous, 6th Congress of Oceanographers?' The person giving the report, having earlier prepared for this question, would answer without hesitation that at the 6th Congress, the delegation was bigger, and that the expense was also significantly larger – as a result of which the permission would be granted. If something was submitted for the Secretariat's review for which there was no precedent – let us say, for example, a conference on the problems of disarmament was to be held for the first time, and with the participation of the Social Democrats – the stock question 'For the first time?' would automatically follow. There would then be a short pause, followed by the customary (and heavy with meaning) 'We have to think about it.' 'To think about it' meant, from Suslov's mouth, that a decision on the question, since there existed no precedent, would not be made by the Secretariat – and that it was useless to argue any further.

I must also mention that Suslov, in his experience, knowledge, and general level of culture, was a head above other secretaries – such as, say, Andrei Kirilenko, or Ivan Kapitonov. He was a master tactician, embodying all the experience and changes in Party policy from Khrushchev to Brezhnev, where he undoubtedly played first violin. It was namely he who, more than the others, worked to chill down 'the thaw', and consign to oblivion everything that had been proclaimed at the 29th Congress of the CPSU. An entire era passed with the death of Suslov, since he was one of the last representatives of the Stalin school, and its heir and continuer in his positions, style, and methods of working.

Time is primarily people and their characters, attitudes, and deeds. The period during which I worked in the CC CPSU and in the newspaper *Sovetskaya Rossiya* can also be described in terms of many sinister figures, which also to a large degree reflected the times – and were a warning of the inevitability of change, and the need to destroy the power of the Party elite. Among the most odious figures of that time, G.S. Pavlov and K.M. Bogoliubov were most visibly set apart by their self-importance and haughtiness. The former was Director of CC CPSU Affairs, and the latter was head of the General Department. These men (the steward and his senior accountant for all incoming and outgoing papers) were, for a quite long time, figures who enjoyed practically unlimited power within the CC CPSU apparatus.

Without their participation and patronage, it was impossible to decide anything within the CC CPSU. It was not only we poor, unimportant chief editors of the central Party newspapers and magazines (which, by the way, brought in the largest portion of Party funds and income) who came into their offices as meek petitioners, humbly requesting help and begging for essential material needs, but also the heads of departments and CC secretaries.

Naturally, when the aristocracy becomes enfeebled and impotent, the time comes for mischief and omnipotence on the part of the servants. To get even with these representatives of Party might, there was nothing that the servants considered too far-fetched or reprehensible. Now running the store, they were in charge of distributing the Party's financial and material wealth – and provided primarily for themselves! They judged their 'laborious and heroic activities' to be extremely important, and thus considered it necessary to award themselves (with the highest approval) the titles of Hero of Socialist Labour and Laureates of the State and Lenin Prizes. Klavdi Bogoliubov considered it perfectly all right for himself to regularly receive in the political press concrete personal author's honours for the collections of documents and materials that were issued by the CC CPSU. Bogoliubov's unique final deed may serve as proof of the complete loss of moral restraints and common decency that was common: his inclusion, by his own hand, in the list of those to be awarded the Order of the Patriotic War as a war veteran, without having served during the war in the slightest. Pavlov, Bogoliubov, and those like them expressed in their lives and actions the shape of their times, and reflected its essence and main features.

The abbreviated period of Yuri Andropov's tenure as First Party Secretary – and as supporter of a harsh system of rule – could not leave any noticeable traces in the CC apparatus's style of work. Andropov's short Party rule turned out to be only potentially threatening, and once again stirred hopes which had long ago been extinguished. There are now many harsh judgements of Andropov, by people from Fyodor Burlatsky to Mikhail Gorbachev.

All these various judgements are characterised by a general striving to paint Yuri Andropov as a person incapable of making radical decisions.

Andropov's short-lived activities as General Secretary of the CPSU still await objective study. I will say now that I do not share the predilection to belittle his role. I think that it is necessary to judge him on the basis of what he himself managed to say, without adding anything. I am thinking here of his famous article, published in the magazine *Kommunist* at the beginning of 1983, *The Study of Karl Marx and Some Questions on The Building of Socialism in the USSR*, and his speech delivered at the plenum of the CC CPSU in June 1983.

In his speeches, the attentive reader may discover an extremely critical attitude towards the achievements of socialism, and for the first time, a statement of the problem of the need to perfect socialism, which represented a historically prolonged stage. In the speech at the plenum, he said even more clearly that 'to speak openly, we still, even now, have not studied to the necessary degree the society in which we live and work...' I think that it is only in these cardinal remarks that it is not difficult to see the basic need for radical change in our society. We cannot be misled by the attempts of Gorbachev, in his interview with *Nezavisimaya gazeta* (November 11,1992), to discredit Andropov, under the not-too-subtle title of 'Andropov Didn't Go Very Far in Reforming Society'.

The greatest changes in the work of the CC CPSU in recent years were connected with the names Mikhail Gorbachev and Yegor Ligachev. These leaders, though they were very different in character, had a great deal in common. It was namely they who, along with the new ideas of glasnost and democratisation, brought as provincials to the CC CPSU apparatus the verbose and bustling style of the regional committees, with their hours-long and loquacious Secretariat sessions, and unending series of different types of deliberations, conferences, meetings, and rallies. It was precisely at that time that the Central Committee held scores of all-Union congresses on various economic issues, complete with tedious and drawn-out monologues by the Central Committee secretaries. As a rule, their reports amounted to little more than propaganda and had little, if any, effect on the economy.

The style of the work of the Central Committee was fast becoming provincial, inefficient and hectic. At that time, in a euphoric perestroika atmosphere accompanied by a feverish search for something else to dismantle and overhaul, were adopted the notorious CC resolution and, soon after, the 'general sobriety' decree of the Presidium of the USSR Supreme Soviet. While the cumbersome Central Committee bureaucracy was pared down and made more democratic, the efficiency of the Party's organisational activities markedly deteriorated in the process. This happened because in their desire to dismantle the old structures and outdated party work methods the new provincial leaders did not propose any constructive alternatives to them, as they had a very dim idea of the objectives and ways of reforming the Party. I am convinced that this set the stage for an inevitable crisis and serious trials for the Communist Party of the Soviet Union in the near future.

The Betrayal and Death of the CPSU

As someone who took part in the last plenary sessions of the

Central Committee and in secretariat meetings, and who sat on CPSU Central Committee commissions, it fell to my lot to personally witness the death-throes of the Communist Party. My time spent at the sharp end of public opinion has convinced me that the more complex and contradictory an event, the greater the caution, circumspection and tolerance that must be shown when it comes to assessing it; furthermore, that due allowance should be given for the fact that different approaches to the analysis of cause and effect are inevitable. Here the reader will guess that I am returning to the question which was raised in the title.

The changes that have taken place in the party in recent years, its internal evolution so to speak, have been the direct result of perestroika. Today everyone – both left and right – are agreed that perestroika was itself the result of the objective necessity to accelerate the social and economic development of Soviet society. And whatever we think of it now, perestroika was inevitable because economic, social, scientific and cultural problems had come to such a head that radical change was required and fundamental decisions had to be made. These changes were initiated by the Party, but that was only to be expected because at the time such an initiative could not have come from anyone else. I agree with N.I.Ryzhkov and some others that the basic ideas behind perestroika were already being discussed as early as 1983 and 1984 on the initiative of Yu.V.Andropov. At the April Plenum of the Central Committee in 1985 and at the 27th Congress of the CPSU in February, 1986, the ideas for accelerating social and economic development were approved and passed as the party policy for restructuring (perestroika) all aspects of Soviet society.

Perestroika was brought about by serious problems, particularly economic problems. Over the previous decade there had been a fall in national income and labour productivity growth rates, which had dropped to 2-3% (as against 6-7% in the previous decade). These slow growth rates were bringing the country to a standstill, because they could not guarantee any improvement in the material well-being of the Soviet people and thus prevented achievement of the country's main social objectives. The worst area, despite all the numerous reforms that had been implemented since the time of Khrushchev, was agricultural production, where harvests were poor and losses amounted to 20-30%. The last attempt at reform – Gorbachev's creation of agro-industrial associations – also proved fruitless. Those less well-disposed to the government at the time ascribed the creation of *Agroprom* with all the billions of roubles spent on maintaining it not to Gorbachev, but to the CIA.

It is easy to be wise after the event. Those who began perestroika had a very poor idea of where it was leading. They looked upon it as the regeneration of Soviet society which would fully realize the potential of the socialist system. In our evaluations – and I would like to draw attention to this – no interest was shown in the fact that perestroika was to a large extent caused by the need to reassess non-material values and rethink many of the ideological stereotypes and dogmas.

Speaking as a person who spent a long time as a professional in this area, I know only too well that while it was customary to refer in words to ideological activity and the material conditions of the people as something unified, in practice ideological activity was always quite divorced from the realities of life, completely independent of economic and social processes. This inevitably resulted in growing contradictions between party propaganda and everyday life, between what was being said and what was really happening. The attempt to resolve this contradiction and tell the truth to the people, which was made at the 20th Congress of the CPSU was shortlived. Those party leaders, who like M.A.Suslov were quite well aware of the difference between words and realities, set out to deliberately exaggerate the effects of ideological activity and gave their full support to vast campaigns in the hope that increases in the size and scale of propaganda would result in the increased effect of ideology on society. There was nothing new about this – it was a method that has been widely used by rulers at all times. But life is the finest teacher, and life taught an infallible lesson – with the result that millions of people began to give less and less credence to the ideas of the Party, for all the intensity of effort that was put into spreading them, because these ideas did not correspond with what the reality of their own experience showed them.

But these increases in the amount of propaganda could not conceal the obvious fact that the Party was not on the same wavelength as those who worked in the arts and the sciences. Education and science fell ever increasingly behind. And none of the bombastic claims or speeches about the welfare of the people could conceal the fact that such vital areas as healthcare, education and culture stood right at the end of the line when it came to matters of financing. Thus it was hardly surprising that the seventies and eighties were marked by revelations of the serious financial difficulties facing culture and the arts. In Moscow alone the majority of theatres, museums and picture galleries were in a state of utter neglect. On the other hand, gigantic structures of stone and marble, whole complexes of buildings like those of the Committee of State Security and the Ministry of Defence costing hundreds of millions of roubles were built at the same time right in the centre of Moscow, almost making it absolutely crystal clear what the real directions of Soviet state policy were. I remember as I used to go about the centre of Moscow how I often used to think about how stupid and shortsighted our Party leadership were in being unable to see and understand what any impartial person would realize at a glance: just what the real priorities in our society, just what was given real care and attention by the Party.

At that time one did not have to be particularly well versed in the ways of the Party to realize that it was facing a crisis. As evidence there were the artificial party membership waiting lists for the intelligentsia, the long, tedious and pointless hours spent at useless party meetings, the practice of granting days off work with double pay for participation in the May Day and October Revolution demonstrations, the years spent in purely formal attendance at political education studies that gave nothing to the mind or the heart, and much else. Other indications that all was not well with the Party, that it was in fact stagnating came from the increasing incidence of party members abusing their positions. Of the 54,000 letters received by the Party Control Commission in 1984 more than 15,000, i.e. one third, referred to cases of bribery, misappropriation and the squandering of resources.

The processes of democratization in the life of Soviet society and the economic and cultural transformations which all took place in 1985 and 1986 went ahead of any changes in the Party itself. This was because the great mass of the Soviet people were already beginning to think and act in a different way, while most of the party workers both in the centre and in the localities remained in the grip of old ideas. They tried to run things in the old way and still relied on the prestige of party power. Those who worked in the party apparatus were unwilling to try and understand what was happening in the country, but particularly they feared the growing public involvement of people, people who thought differently and who were not submissive.

Sharply differing attitudes to the changes in society began increasingly to appear at the plenary sessions of the Central Committee. One of the first of such plenary sessions was that held in October, 1987. The agenda stipulated matters connected with the 70th anniversary of the October Revolution, but the debates turned to something quite different, with the result that the session achieved wide notoriety for the rebellious behaviour of Boris Yeltsin in sharply criticizing the Secretariat and the Politburo. His harsh criticisms were directed against Yegor Ligachov, as head of the Secretariat, for failing to change the old command style of running the party committees and for the ill-considered and inconsistent decisions taken by the Party. Yeltsin's speech boiled down to the demand that the Party should at long last begin restructuring the work of the party committees and the Party as a whole from the Secretariat downwards. His criticisms were unusual but fair, because commands and directives to restructure the forms and methods of party work did indeed continue to predominate in party practice, even though nothing actually got changed at all. And evidence of the fact that little had changed, after prolonged talks in the Party on the need for democratic reform, was shown quite clearly in the reaction to Yeltsin's speech. This natural and justified example of dissent in a party that had itself proclaimed democracy and glasnost was not accepted. The attitude of the party leaders to criticism was unashamedly negative and contained elements of open hostility and irritation. The replies to Yeltsin contained the same old accusations of immaturity, demagogy, and the putting of personal interests above those of the Party.

As one who was present at the October Plenum, I have to admit, that the condemnation expressed by all the members of the Politburo and the Central Committee, albeit in a friendly tone, aroused my annoyance – and not mine alone. Their speeches contained one theme and one only: 'How dare you speak like that!' There was not the slightest desire to listen to his arguments or understand the thrust of his criticism. It made me start to worry that to all intents and purposes nothing in the party had changed; the same tight centralism remained, the same lack of democracy.

But I'm not saying simply what I think now long after the event. It so happened two days after the Central Committee Plenum that I requested a meeting with A.N.Yakovliev to discuss some matters regarding the press and book-publishing. I can remember quite well that at the end of this conversation Yakovliev, who was always interested to know the opinions of his comrades, asked me what I thought about the decision of the Plenum on Yeltsin and whether it should have been different. I think there was a purpose in his asking me, because he had been wondering about it himself, although like the others he had condemned Yeltsin in his speech to the Plenum. I made no attempt to hide my concern over such absolute refusal to accept Yeltsin's criticisms and made the point that such harsh condemnation of Yeltsin did nothing for the prestige of the Central Committee. I said that if I had my way, I would not have tried to make him into a dissident. Yakovliev agreed with me, but added that given the present composition of the Central Committee, no other decision was possible. I realize that all this was easier to say in a personal conversation than from the Plenum tribune.

As a delegate attending the 19th Party Conference, I have to admit that I found the difference between it and all the previous conferences, congresses and plenums quite striking for the unprecedented frankness of the debates and the heated nature of the arguments. The tone was set by a number of newcomers who brought with them radically new ideas and a completely fresh approach. The speeches made at the conference by two workers, Yarin from Nizhni Tagil and Nizhelevsky from Orsk, by Aidak from Chuvashia and Kabaidze from Ivanovo, both economists, and by Yelizarov and Fyodorov, two medical students made them immediately popular throughout the country. Contrasted with this were the dull, boring, thought-numbing discourses of the party workers, most of whom were hardly listened to and some of whom, like the Moscow Party Secretary, Belyaninov, were booed off the tribune. The speeches of the Central Committee Secretaries from

Armenia (Arutunyan), Azerbaijan (Vezirov) and Moldova (Grossu) were completely featureless. But there were rare exceptions, like Melnikov, First Secretary of the Regional Committee of the Komi Republic, who spoke frankly about the conservatism and political backwardness of the Politburo and who, when Gorbachev tried to trap him, named the names of some of the highest men in the Politburo, like Gromyko, Vorotnikov and Slyunkov referring to them as 'yesterday's men'.

The last attempt of the Party to take the initiative and avert the crisis came during the drafting of the new CPSU Programme. On July 25 and 26 the Central Committee held its last Plenum, which approved the new draft programme for subsequent broad discussion in the Party. At the same time it was also decided to call an extraordinary 29th Congress of the CPSU for November-December, 1991. But although the new draft Programme made radical reforms to the CPSU, turning it into a social-democratic parliamentary party, it was unable to surmount the growing contradictions within the party. A large part of the party apparatus refused to approve it and spoke vehemently against it.

In these conditions no amount of broad discussion could change the situation inside the CPSU. At a time of acute social crisis, sharply falling production, economic mismanagement and the impotence of the central executive powers, nationwide discussion of the party programme, which had come far too late, could only give rise to increasing indignation among the people, especially since most people saw the CPSU as the prime cause of all the country's problems. The time that had been lost was wreaking its vengeance. It was no longer possible to restore lost confidence in the Party. For this reason the unjust and undemocratic decision to ban the Party aroused no serious opposition from communists and non-communists alike. No public demonstrations were made of any importance. And this, however hard it is to admit, is the most serious argument in support of the claim that the Party was not killed off, it just committed suicide.

Chapter 3 – 'Sweet Hell':
Eight Years at *Sovetskaya Rossiya*

Journalists nowadays are often flattered with the label 'the fourth branch of government' (i.e. fourth in seniority after the executive, legislative and judicial wings) – when they are reminded that they are members of 'the second oldest profession' they are somewhat less enthusiastic. But both these definitions share common ground: journalists play the tune of those who pay for the music, and they are perennially dependent on the powers that be. We have rid ourselves of many illusions. The experience of the last few years has significantly enriched us, particularly with an understanding of the evolution that our press has undergone: from the dictate of the Party to the euphoria of 'glasnost', and back again to the old dependence on those in power, only this time partly disguised with slogans about democracy and freedom of thought.

I was fortunate to take part at the beginning of this evolution, when the press was trying to overcome its slavish obedience and was learning to tell the truth. This was a difficult period in which it regained its dignity and the right to be itself, the right to serve the people and not those in power. Ten years on I can see that much of what occupied our thoughts and which at the time we so laboured to overcome is once again on the agenda, since the press is again expected to be an obedient servant – not of the reader, but of the ruling élite.

Getting Started

After my third year in the propaganda department of the Central Committee I had understood that work in the Party apparatus with its regime of obedience and its close grip of dependency was not for me. I began to think of work that might bring a relative degree of freedom. As it happened, my thoughts unexpectedly coincided with those of the head of the department.

Six years after the 25th Congress of the CPSU, a figure to run the Central Committee's propaganda and agitation department was at last appointed. M.V. Zimyanin, former editor of *Pravda*, was chosen to be the secretary to the Central Committee responsible for propaganda matters, and Ye.M. Tyazhelnikov was soon after appointed to head the department.

Without more ado the new chief set about assembling his team. With obedience of subordinates the top priority, he began to enact his intentions principally through appointment of new deputy heads. Tyazhelnikov and I were well acquainted, so I knew very well that I couldn't count on his support for my hopes of independence. My premonitions were swiftly confirmed. As soon as the opportunity arose to suggest a new editor for *Sovetskaya Rossiya* (Soviet Russia) from within the department, he put my name forward without even consulting me. I only learnt of the recommendation from Zimyanin when he called me in and asked me to think the proposal over.

Now that this is all history I am glad that it happened this way and that Tyazhelnikov was not particularly enamoured with me. He probably understood my negative attitude to his methods. His loyal pronouncements heaping praise on Brezhnev's good works earned him the reputation of 'the great leader's' outstanding mouthpiece, and were enough to strike dumb even the most experienced of Central Committee apparatchiks. Let God be his judge. His decision was a boon for me, and for this I am grateful to him.

Among the various meetings at the time I remember a conversation with Konstantin Zarodov, the main editor of *Sovetskaya Rossiya* and a man of wisdom who had done much to get the paper established. He did not hide the difficulties and potential dangers of my future appointment. A major factor, which he believed I would be unable to do anything about, was the diversity of the journalistic corpus. Its various components were as follows, he said: the first layer, consisting of creative individuals who compile the newspaper and contribute interesting and sensational material, create new columns and so on, is small on any newspaper – some 10 or 15% of the staff; the second layer is slightly larger, 20-30%, and includes those who, to the best of their usually modest capabilities, produce the main bulk of material without which the newspaper cannot exist; and the third and final layer, usually the largest at some 50% of the staff, who make a minor input but actively obstruct the work of producing the newspaper. These are mainly people with big egos and ambitions but with little creative ability, almost completely useless. Many of them are either doing what they are not suited for, or have simply exhausted what little creative reserve they may have had.

There are many people who fit this description, and they don't only work on newspapers. They usually make a big show of doing something, but constantly get in the way, endlessly talking about the lack of facilities or creative freedom, quarrelling and intriguing with those who are really being creative and trying to do something useful. This sterile group of journalists usually numbers many critics of the newspaper and its stand. It issues plenty of statements of creative intent, but without having any real creativity to draw upon. Given his own experience, Zarodov advised me not to waste energy and not to try to get rid of these layers – not only is it impossible, but it would take up so much time that there would be none left for the paper itself. In his opinion the chief editor should know how to neutralise the sterile layer, limit its influence and, if possible, shift the balance of forces towards the first, creative layer.

New appointments, even after talking to the Central Committee secretary, took a long time to be put into effect and went through a long clearing process in the Secretariat and the Politburo. The editor of a national Party newspaper was *nomenklatura* in the top flight of the Party. It took two months before I was told the Politburo's decision and on April 7, 1978, I was introduced to the newspaper staff.

While I was making my first steps at the paper the Soviet press was going through troubled times. It could not be otherwise. The press mirrored the general political, social and spiritual atmosphere of a society in prolonged stagnation and in which any talk of change or reform was rejected by the upper Party echelons. The Party's official position which the press was required to affirm expressed the mood of self-satisfied complacency in the ruling elite and consisted of hymns to prosperity and well-being throughout society and the indestructible might and authority of Party and government.

To the limit of their professional abilities, knowledge, commitment and loyalty the papers repeated this official position in millions upon millions of copies.

As a result of these basic circumstances, and not through lack of talent (our country has never lacked talented people), the papers did not stand out for the variety and brightness of their journalistic palettes, for their militant and critical stance, let alone for any opposition to what was happening in the real world. The last critical upsurge at newspapers such as *Komsomolskaya pravda* (Komsomol Truth) or *Izvestia* (The News), reflecting the contradictions in the Khrushchev thaw and the high hopes of reform among the intelligentsia after the 20th Party Congress, had long since evaporated like a dream.

Just as every period has its loud supporters and popularisers, the Brezhnev stagnation also had its propagandists and ideologists. It is unfortunate that now, when the past is everywhere subjected to frenzied denunciation, we are insufficiently self-critical and reluctant to admit that the mass media must take a substantial share of the blame for all those declarations of universal prosperity, coming at a time when society needed to be warned of the imminent misfortunes that were knocking so insistently at the door. As critics of authority like to say, 'the country must know its heroes'. But it was the papers and magazines, radio and television, particularly in the last ten years of Brezhnev's rule, that maintained the mood of loyalty and obedience, actively created the illusion of prosperity and glossed over the evidence that the country had long been living beyond its means. Journalists cannot deny their responsibility: the triumphal drum roll emitting from the printed page and TV screen had the effect of soothing public opinion and drowning out the voices of those who were trying to bring attention to the fact that society was seriously unwell.

In the 1970s the achievements of the press were far from outstanding, and very few publications were exceptions to the rule. Each newspaper bowed to the existing, immutable order and lived according to its particular rank and the corresponding support it received from the Party at both national and local level. The activities and development of the press met fully with the demands of Party hegemony. As a result there was a stable, fixed minimum of national and local publications and there were large obstacles in the way of anything new. The large circulation and uncontested leadership of the big national papers largely determined the limited choice of periodicals for the Soviet reader. Behind each publication stood rigid Party, state and social structures that guaranteed influence and a fixed volume of subscriptions.

At the time when I was trying to come to terms with my role as editor, the general atmosphere was such that the top priority was obedience and an ability to produce only what was wanted and allowed. This was regulated by strict selection of editors-in-chief and through the mechanism of rigid control by the Central Committee's propaganda department. To this end the department's deputy head, the watchful Vladimir Sevruk, and the newspaper section with a dozen or so instructors personally scrutinised the national newspapers with a sleepless eye, closely and passionately assessing each new issue for its loyalty to the Party.

The selection of editors-in-chief was usually made on the basis of the personal acquaintance and trust of the secretaries to the Central Committee, and usually from the people who had commended themselves by their suitable behaviour. Only then were talent and professionalism taken into account as secondary factors. For this reason the editors-in-chief of the national press were rarely chosen from among the editorial staff. As far as I am aware, that was almost unheard of among such major publications as *Pravda*, *Izvestia*, *Trud* (Labour), *Selskaya zhizn* (Rural Life) and *Sovetskaya kultura* (*Soviet Culture*). Given this practice, the following paradox was inevitable: the lesser the creative abilities of the editor appointed by the CC, the greater were his chances of success. An example of this was the phenomenon of Pyotr Alekseyev, well-known in the newspaper world, who was editor of *Selskaya zhizn*, *Sovetskaya Rossiya* and *Izvestia*, and who left each newspaper in ruins. This was not merely a person devoid of creative potential: he was a master of court intrigue, a subtle tactician who knew how to turn empty propaganda slogans into newspaper articles so as to win the highest favour of the Party leadership. At the time that I am talking about he had already destroyed *Sovetskaya Rossiya*, reducing it to the level of a mediocre wall newspaper, and had been sent on the highest authority to reform *Izvestia*, which he rapidly transformed into something quite unrecognisable. In no time at all the paper was full of loud headlines in huge letters announcing banal appeals and slogans such as: *Direct All Forces to the Struggle Against Milkless Cows!*, *We Must Nobly Prepare for the Spring Sowing!*, and so on. I once met Alekseyev when seeking advice from more experienced colleagues in the national press. He remarked that one should be able to read a newspaper with one's legs: the big bosses read nothing but the headlines. He produced newspapers for the top leadership, while the ordinary reader interested him least of all.

When Alekseyev at last relieved *Sovetskaya Rossiya* of his editorial attentions the newspaper was in a sorry state. Founded in 1956 on the wave of Khrushchev's reforms as a paper for Russia (specifically the organ of the Central Committee bureau for the Russian Federation), in its early stages it stood out for paying less attention to Moscow officialdom and more to the Russian provinces. Readers were attracted by its criticism of injustice and the inefficiency of the local leaders that dominated Russian provincial life. In the brief four-year period of his editorship, Alekseyev had done much to destroy the paper. Many of its most interesting journalists had left, there was no place on its pages for criticism and serious analytical material, as a result of which the circulation had dropped by half and stood at about a million copies.

I do not want the reader to think that I am intentionally painting an excessively gloomy picture of the life and ethics of Soviet journalism at the time. Neither am I exaggerating or glossing over anything to suit the present conjuncture; I am telling it as I saw and understood the situation given my own personal views and predilections. More important, I believe, is the question that nags me constantly: is it really useful and necessary to go over the recent past once again? This is for the reader to judge. Here I will merely say that the past is now behind us, but that it contains the answer to the question: what is happening to the mass media and where are they going?

Today we are all preoccupied with the question of why the road from Party dictate to glasnost and independence is so long and difficult for the press, radio and television. Why does so much of what we see today in the press remind us of something cast from the mould of our recent and rejected past? So much is being repeated, but simply on another twist of the spiral. There are many questions. I cherish the hope that the reader will find answers to some of them in these reminiscences of a former editor.

Frequently have I heard journalists remark that working on a newspaper is sweet hell. Only when I became editor did I grasp the deep significance of this phrase, which I understand to refer to the fact that, despite all the complexities of the newspaper profession, it gives one not only the satisfaction of creative work, but also the chance to see its results. I doubt there is any other line of work that enables you to see in print the following morning that which you wrote today, and to find out in person whether the material evoked a favourable reaction from the public or was rejected out of hand. The advantage of a newspaper is that it forces one like no other occupation to be constantly right at the epicentre of current events, at the sharp end of the contradictions and conflicts of daily life – the newspaper is their reflection.

The Editor's Sweet Sorrow

No. 24 Pravda Street will stay in my memory for the rest of my life. At this address I spent 8 years filled to the brim with interesting work and active life, joy and sorrow, victories and defeats. The editorial offices of *Sovetskaya Rossiya* were situated at the time on the 5th floor of this, the largest press building in Moscow. It was an incredible structure, somewhat reminiscent of an enormous cake, the filling between its many layers provided by the editorial offices of some of the best-known national papers. On the 6th floor *Sovetskaya Rossiya* was next door to *Komsomolskaya pravda*, whose impudence and daring didn't give us a moment's peace, while downstairs were the official flag-ship *Pravda* and *Selskaya zhizn*, influential among agricultural workers. At the time the inhabitants of this rather unique institution got along without particular friction, though constantly watching each other with a jealous eye: not a single statement of any note went unnoticed by the other editorials.

Editors are usually divided into two groups: the daring, capable of major deeds, and the timid, totally dependent on the powers that be. One often hears the view that there is no such thing as a courageous journalist, but only courageous editors who bear the responsibility for whether or not a particular article sees the light of day. Although there is more than a grain of truth in this, I can't help saying that it somewhat oversimplifies the situation. I am sure the reader will agree: the idea of 'courageous journalism' has little in common with bravura, with the often spontaneous, individual act of courage. A daring and risky deed such as saving a drowning person is clearly a different matter. When we talk about courage in journalism, we mean bravery of another sort. Here one does not merely have to overcome oneself, one's own natural fear and weakness: this is the life-long courage of everyday professional life with its duties and commitments. I don't believe in spontaneity and improvised free-thinking, for I know very well that every serious political step taken by a newspaper is inevitably preceded by the question: what are we doing this for?

To maintain a steady grip, an editor must be certain that he is producing a newspaper that people need. The main source of this certainty is readers' letters. In order to keep a finger constantly on the pulse of readers' opinions, we set up a special sociological service at *Sovetskaya Rossiya*, based on the experience of *Komsomolskaya pravda* and *Literaturnaya gazeta* but attempting to go still further towards understanding our readership. The main argument in defence of sociology is its usefulness to the paper itself: the opportunity to get answers from readers to a range of editorial questions in the space of a week. This gives a convincing rebuff to journalistic complacency, widespread even today, which assumes that we know everything about our readers without the assistance of sociology. Readers' letters were the main material for our sociological service. To the extent to which *Sovetskaya Rossiya* increasingly concerned the reader, directly addressing his interests, so the number of letters grew. In 1978 there were only a little over 30,000 letters, but by 1985 this had risen to 200,000.

Readers' letters did not merely increase our certainty; they were also the newspaper's sternest critics. Not even the tiniest mistake or ill-chosen remark escaped the readers' observant eyes. It is always with a sense of wonder that I recall these letters, which were the source of such sweet sorrow for the editor. One particular example confirms just how attentive and meticulous was the readership of *Sovetskaya Rossiya*. For March 8, 1984, International Women's Day, we asked several well-known writers and actors who supported the paper to say a few words. Anatoly Papanov, a good friend of *Sovetskaya Rossiya* and a well-known performer, wrote the following: 'It was Prosper Merimée who said that a woman is always beautiful: both on the bridal couch and on her death bed.' A week later we received a letter addressed to the editor, which contained the following: 'Your women's page was interesting, but unfortunately not without mistakes. I have in mind the piece by Papanov. The words he quoted are not those of Merimée, but of Ovid, who actually said something very different: "A woman is beautiful only twice: once on the bridal couch and once on her death bed."' We checked the quote and found that the reader was right.

Readers' letters and our sociological service helped the paper establish a dialogue with the readership which continued for many years. This became the paper's bedrock and enabled us to raise the circulation every year by over 500,000: in 1978 circulation was about 1 million, and by 1985 it had climbed to over 4 million.

From the very moment one sits in the editor's chair and the phone rings, one must learn to carry the heavy burden of responsibility for the paper on one's own shoulders. There are many positions of responsibility, some of which I have experienced for myself, but I know of no other to compare with editing a newspaper for its daily demands to take responsibility on oneself.

The concept of 'technological risk' is well-established. But I believe that the concept of 'journalistic risk' should be more widely recognised. This describes what happens in those instances when the editor takes a conscious decision to take a stand in print, with full knowledge of the risk of defeat and its consequences. I know from my own experience that such a step is usually dictated by the conviction that it is socially necessary, the paper's public duty. An example of this kind of risk was the series of articles by our special correspondent Vitaly Avdevich in the summer of 1985 on the serious condition of the Moscow construction sector, the instance of 'dressing up' and inflating its real achievements. One could predict beforehand that these materials would meet with categorical rejection and resistance from the city administration, led by the first secretary of the City Party Committee, Politburo member Viktor Grishin, and that he would set powerful forces against the newspaper. That is exactly what happened. There was pressure on me from all sides, including direct threats to 'sort out' the editor. The propaganda department of the Central Committee, led by M.V. Zimyanin, immediately turned its fire on the paper. The main argument was a traditional one and did not concern the real content of the articles. How, it was argued, could the capital, a city of 'exemplary communist labour', be shown in such an unfavourable light? The decision to publish the material was a risk for *Sovetskaya Rossiya*, but an inevitable one if it wanted to remain honest and principled. Of course, such a risk demands the absolute certainty of the editor that his journalist won't let him down and won't fail to tell the truth.

Among such risky articles which inevitably led to conflict I would number the piece by Vladimir Yakovlev, *The Claque*, which described the unfortunate condition of the Bolshoi Theatre in Moscow, considered by the press at that time to be quite beyond criticism. There was a similar reaction to our critical reviews of the 1984 Moscow tour by the Leningrad Drama Theatre under Georgy Tovstonogov, also considered safe from objective criticism in the press. I could name many more articles – there was one in practically every issue – which could be considered risky, in which the paper took a stand for truth and justice.

In pondering the editor's difficult role, I come to a question that I am often asked: do I regret leaving the newspaper and would I not have preferred to remain there? The job of editor has no equal in terms of the intense pace of work, the constant need to be in good shape and fully geared to a rapid assimilation of what is taking place. Thus I do not believe that one can remain in such a post for very long. Every individual has his own capacity for work, but no one's resources are unlimited or inexhaustible. Given that this is the case, there is inevitably potential to slip gradually into a routine and to conform to set stereotypes, which can prove to be very hard to get away from. There is nothing more harmful to a newspaper than habitual themes, columns, presentation and layout. In order to find the strength to make major changes, rid oneself of stereo-types and reassess editorial criteria one needs a fresh point of view – that of a new editor. This is my answer to the question posed above, and it is fully borne out in practice. The dismal uniformity of so many newspapers perpetuated in the past was to a great extent the result of the long reign of one and the same editor.

The time has not yet come, I believe, to give a detailed charac-terisation of the basic stages through which the Soviet press has gone on the road from Party dictate to glasnost. However, some aspects of the Soviet Union's final two or three years, and the state of the press in 1992 in conditions of officially sanctioned demo-cracy, are already clear.

The democratic period in perestroika was marked by a huge growth in the social influence of the mass media. But like any other period, this was a contradictory one. By the end of 1989 the contradiction was becoming more and more obvious: on the one hand, there was the unheard-of popularity of the press, and on the other, the progressive increase in readers' complaints and criticism from left and right, from above and from below. When one con-siders this paradox, one sees that the contradiction was the inevi-table child of contradictory times, a reflection of the complexity of the processes under way in society at a sharp turning-point in its development. Economic, political and ethnic contradictions were stretched to the limit – they were tearing society apart, sowing confusion, doubt and loss of faith in the road to reform. I think that this period was particularly difficult for those who were profes-sionally involved with the press – it was tough enough to be a contemporary of those difficult times, but it was three times as tough to go through it all and reflect it in one's difficult role as chronicler.

There are those who maintain that the concept of the basic function of the press as reflecting everything that is happening in real life served to seriously weaken the connection between the Party and the mass media. In particular, Yegor Ligachev in his book, *The Gorbachev Enigma* devoted much attention to the nega-tive effects of this so-called 'reflection theory'.

To my mind, this point of view partially expresses the old and unprofessional approach to the press as obedient mouthpiece of the Party. I believe that the rejection of such an approach led to the recognition that the main role of the press is indeed to reflect processes and events in real life. No matter how much we may argue, it is precisely facts and real events that are the main focus of the press, television and radio, and not the directives of Party and state authorities.

Here I cannot help giving my opinion concerning the objectivity or bias, the dependence or independence of the media. There is constant polemic on this theme in the press, on television and radio, and there is much confusion, extremism and frequent assertions that the media are clearly lacking in objectivity. But if one attempts sensibly to define what objectivity is in practice, one is forced to admit that it is but the principle in which the journalist's subjective position is expressed, it is always the generator of his views and interests. This also concerns the frequent assertions about press independence. Each newspaper or magazine staff lives and works in real conditions within an immense web of various connections, relations and a multitude of dependencies – economic, social, political, spiritual – and the journalist is free and independent only within the limits of these views, goals and interests, because his dependence on his own convictions and preferences is just as real as any other dependence. The statement that independence is just as impossible as a perpetual motion machine is not without foundation, and it accords with the objective laws of social life. It is a different matter when independence is taken to mean recognition of opposing points of view, tolerance, and fearlessness in the face of criticism from those who do not share the editorial board's position.

If one takes a closer look, one can discern another aspect to the current voluminous discussions about independence. Waving the flag of press independence, there are also the pragmatists and opportunists who, in their own purely commercial interest, enthusiastically promote anything that was once forbidden, even pornography, and mask their actions in a fog of 'innovation' and 'freedom of thought'. Observation shows that what we have here is a massive attack of Philistines who are successfully conquering one position after another in the mass media, literature, the theatre and cinema, playing on the fact that most journalists, writers and publicists are wary of being accused of dogma and conservatism and keep silent in the face of this total assault of vulgarity and banality.

Democracy and glasnost have undoubtedly given a great impulse to the activities of the press, whose authority and social influence have grown to unheard-of dimensions. Its achievements in its difficult battle for glasnost were given legislative foundation in the Law on the Press and Information. Ratified by the USSR Supreme Soviet in 1990, the law stimulated those new processes that were becoming more and more apparent in the press. In 1990-91 a mass of new newspapers and magazines appeared. In Moscow in 1991 over 3,000 periodicals were registered, half of them new. The structure also changed: no longer did state and Party publications predominate, but those of associations, joint ventures and charitable foundations. A number of private publications also appeared – over 300 in Moscow alone.

The press was typically in opposition to the government at this time. The question of the legitimacy of this stance is always relevant and deserves a few words. As is already known, during the first stage of perestroika, when the press was mapping out the road to change, it was essentially the only oppositional force in society. It was a necessary opposition, in the sense that it expressed the interests not of one social group or movement but reflected life in all its fullness and with all its contradictions, points of view, and the interests of various categories of workers. When under Stalin we destroyed the content of the dialectic, leaving of this well-known law of the unity and struggle of opposites nothing but the acknowledgment of unity, society lost the main generator of its development. The task of the press, as I see it, is to reflect the great variety of social contradictions, the range of different perceptions and assessments, and to make them accessible to public opinion. One can have different attitudes, but the press will always be necessary – also in its function as a social irritant. I understand that it is most unpleasant to read day after day about deficits, inflation, poverty, tragic ethnic conflicts, about the economic and other problems that are buffeting society. But these are the bitter realities of life today, they are the reality.

After seven years of democratic reform, the country is even further from achieving the intentions, the high-sounding social programmes, that it announced at the beginning.

Discontent among the readership became particularly apparent in 1991 and 1992 when the economic crisis deepened, the Union collapsed and social instability reached extremes. The unheard-of price rises and the fall in living standards of a significant number of the population to subsistence levels increased readers' critical attitude to the press, which they saw as mainly to blame for their misfortunes (it was the press that initiated perestroika). This growing irritation among the readership was one of the main reasons for the sharp fall in the circulation of newspapers and magazines in these years. I believe that this process has yet to reach its limit and will continue, since its cause is not to be found in market relations alone, but also in the rising cost of paper and delivery.

In 1992 the deepening contradiction between the mass media on the one hand and the readers and viewers on the other became even more apparent also because of the diminishing quality of glasnost, the lack of objectivity in the press, radio and TV, which increasingly revealed in their reports and analysis their bias and tendentiousness in carrying out the orders of the ruling political élite. This is a serious worry for professional journalists today who have to their own surprise suddenly seen the strange and unexpected results of the democratisation of the mass media. Among the many observations, typical is the article by V. Nadein, deputy editor of *Izvestia*, in *Moscow News* of May 1992. Here he gives a very precise assessment of the current condition of the press, stressing above all the political predilection of all the papers from *Izvestia* to *Kuranty* (The Chimes – the Moscow daily). 'Our mass media's greatest sin,' writes Nadein, 'is its peculiar attraction to those in power, its constant attention to a narrow circle of one and the same people. And it makes no difference whether they criticise or praise these people: the important thing is that everything revolves around them – the rest is a vacuum.'

Readers have picked up on press bias and argue that the latter's evolution has nothing to do with a true commitment to democracy and glasnost. It is hard to deny readers' conclusions that they know in advance the content of such newspapers as *Izvestia*, *Moskovsky komsomolets* and *Kuranty*, which openly seek to defend the ruling regime.

As a minister who has suffered so much criticism from those calling for press freedom, the current situation reminds me somewhat of an Aesop fable. A wolf once saw shepherds eating a sheep in their tent. The wolf went up to them and said: 'Just think what would happen if I were to do that.' What was once thought impermissible in relations between the government and the press has now become a common phenomenon.

In these contradictory circumstances, suggestions that the press has become 'the fourth branch of government' look strange indeed. It has certainly become a power in society – but whose? If total subservience to the political forces who are running the country can serve as a basic definition of power, then indeed our press has become a power in its own right. This is beyond dispute. A broad cross-section of society has witnessed the most unexpected but rapid transformation of the majority of newspaper, magazine, radio and television editorial boards from yesterday's defenders of free speech and independence into today's obedient and energetic propaganda organs for the powers that be. It is clear to many that the current Russian government went through its period of democratic euphoria in relation to the press when it was still first and foremost in opposition to the centre and the Soviet president. Now everything has returned to its previous orbit, and speeches by those responsible for publishing policy include familiar platitudes: democracy is not freedom to do anything you please, glasnost does not mean wild and indiscriminate behaviour. As a past editor-in-chief, when I come across similar statements – for so long so well-known to us all – I think about what has happened since.

Analysing the press, one notices a clear degradation in the quality of glasnost. This is manifest in the fact that the newspapers are losing their main informative function and are turning into vehicles of political manipulation and banality. In the majority of newspapers and magazines, the struggle of political elites in the highest organs of power are at the centre of attention. This drop in glasnost and professionalism I also see in the rapid formation (obviously a result of old habits) of a significant layer of journalists – particularly in newspapers that are openly subservient to the ruling regime – who repeat the same old themes and choose as objects for their attacks those formerly in power or who have fallen out of favour with the new leadership.

I do not believe that all this is simply a sign of the times: social life is politicised in the extreme, as is the press. But by this I mean not merely the desire to satisfy demand, but the ever-increasing ambition on the part of those who work in this field, who are inclined to think that they have a monopoly on public opinion and can therefore do anything they please. This arrogance assumes the old and accustomed unthinking compliance of the readership and its readiness to accept only what the press itself is prepared to give it. The reader is defenceless and deprived of his rights before the press, just as before.

To me this arrogance is the most dangerous and unpleasant feature of the mass media, its neglect of its own audience, the people, on whom and only on whom the media should depend. I say this with a sense of alarm: I increasingly come across articles in the press which in one way or another assert that each nation deserves to live in the way that it does, and that it deserves its leaders. It is obviously implied that each nation also has the mass media that it deserves. There are countless articles in our press that report with extraordinary relish that we are on a ship full of madmen, a country full of fools. There are endless, tiresome descriptions of the common man as 'rabble', 'cattle', etc. It is hard to deny, of course, that underhand political practice is a widespread social phenomenon. Many of our contemporaries have turned politics into both an art and a profession for achieving unheard-of individual enrichment – evidence of the degradation of both politics and politicians. In this sense one cannot disagree that politicians are only as good as the system of government. But are ordinary people to blame for this? Perhaps only in as much as they show such extraordinary tolerance and meekly permit the politicians to carry out vicious social experiments upon them.

At this point I shall cease in my comments on the present condition of the press and answer an unavoidable question: what do I think about *Sovetskaya Rossiya* today?

The paper now is different in both content and appearance. I understand that this is inevitable, since the life of the paper is now very different. It is satisfying to see that *Sovetskaya Rossiya* has its own position, its own character, and thereby stands out from among the other papers. I don't wish to impose my own point of view, but I believe that one of the sources of its opposition to the current regime is the paper's position in the mid-1980s. As for the turning point, this, I think, was Nina Andreyeva's well-known article of March 19, 1988, *I Cannot Renounce My Principles*, and the sharp criticism of this article that followed in *Pravda*. As we know already, this country has accumulated plenty of experience in the rapid appearance of dissidents. With glasnost and pluralism officially proclaimed, the sharp and categorical criticism of *Sovetskaya Rossiya* hastened the development of a negative attitude on behalf of the editorial board to the General Secretary and his close supporters, and assisted in the formation of *Sovetskaya Rossiya* as the oppositional newspaper that it is today.

I do not share Nina Andreyeva's urge to depict the past history of the Soviet Communist Party as beyond reproach, and I do not think that calls for a return to the past can help the country. But this certainly does not mean that such thunderous and categorical criticism of *Sovetskaya Rossiya* was justified. And today, when the dead-end of perestroika is yet more obvious, one can go further and say that Nina Andreyeva's article could have served to generate fruitful and necessary polemic over goals, means and methods.

Without concealing anything, I would like to say that I cannot help admiring the courage of *Sovetskaya Rossiya*'s current editorial board – all the more so since the cost of their stand has been so high. The paper's voice in defence of our humiliated country has become a fact of social life and no one can ignore it. Fairness demands that I add that the paper's scope and authority would be higher if its pages were open to a wider spectrum of opinions and analyses of current social processes and movements. I also believe that, even in the fiercest polemic, one must not support the idea that defence of one's own position makes anything permissible, including articles on the wives of past and present presidents. Such methods are indefensible, even if they correspond to those of one's opponents, because for a serious newspaper there is a real danger of crossing the line beyond which one is in conflict with the rules and norms of decency.

Against the background of all the contradictions, conflicts and emotions that fill the press today, in conclusion I must return once again to the question of why this talk of the old *Sovetskaya Rossiya* is necessary and can we compare its practical experience with our current worries and concerns.

The test of time is a serious one – not all of us can withstand it. Much of what we discovered for ourselves at *Sovetskaya Rossiya* seems now of minor significance. Every period has its newspapers, just as it has its songs. The period on the eve of radical social change produced *Sovetskaya Rossiya* in the form that I have described above.

Perhaps our experience is modest, perhaps it was just one small step for the press on its road to the present day, but it is valuable and useful as social experience, as the narrow bridge across which the newspapers of today can go further. This experience is at the same time a warning of the real danger that the press can once again return to where it began, to the service not of the truth or the reader but of the ruling political élite. The main lesson to be learnt from *Sovetskaya Rossiya* is that only serving the reader can make a newspaper independent of the political conjuncture, able to adopt a responsible position and influence public opinion. The lesson is also that there is nothing harder than for the slave to overcome the subservience within him. The media's difficult and contradictory road to glasnost and democracy, followed by their journey back and their resulting crisis, is evidence that these lessons are highly relevant today.

Chapter 4 –
The Publishing Business:
My Last Love

The years I spent working in book publishing (1986-88) coincided with an exceptional rise in Russia in the popularity and authority of the printed word. This was provoked by the democratic reforms of perestroika, which, based on glasnost, was in full flower at the time. I do not know if there will ever be such a period again when the press, radio and television are so powerful and enjoy such enormous authority among the people. Articles by publicists and journalists, writers and academics enjoyed unprecedented popularity. Countrywide newspapers, journals and books which had long gone unpublished, including works of banned Russian authors, made themselves heard in numerous copies. The cause of this publishing boom was the emancipation, through perestroika, of writers and readers who had acquired the opportunity to satisfy their need to speak out and learn about Russia's past and present in truthful and unfettered words.

In these unusual circumstances the state publishing system was not capable of satisfying the requirements of the Soviet people for many types of literature, above all fiction, children's books and reference texts. There were many serious reasons influencing the dire shortage of book publications. One of the main ones was the long-time monopoly of the state publishing houses and the total lack of any alternative publishing organisations in Russia: there were no cooperative or private publishing companies. The system of controlling publishing and printing potential also had negative consequences. Striking proof of this shortage was the sharp difference between that which was being published in state publishing houses and what people wanted to buy in bookshops.

Book publishing is a complex business and assessing the processes involved in it is not easy. In essence, the shortage about which I have been speaking was in no way a simple matter. Observations showed the presence of a substantial discrepancy between the shortage in books consumers wished to obtain and the shortage in reading as such. It has been correctly noted that in order to carry out greater reforms three conditions are prerequisite as a minimum: great aims, large obstacles and great examples. As far as large obstacles are concerned, this condition existed in Soviet book publishing, since publishing reflected the contents of conflicting social and spiritual processes operating in society and directly depended on them. For many years reforms had been knocking insistently at the doors of the publishing houses. Everything we softly termed 'stagnation phenomena' had penetrated deep into the publishing business. The book profession was adapted to the conditions of rigid centralism, which were based on administrative hierarchy and obedience. It would be difficult to name another department where in its relations with *Staraya Ploshchad* (the seat of the CC) the principle of 'whatever you say' operated so smoothly. Obviously, the *Goskomizdat* (USSR State Committee for Publishing, Printing and Book Trading) did not have the right nor sufficient material means to conduct an independent publishing policy and was in many respects only the executor of the publishing decisions and directives adopted by the CC and issued through the department of propaganda.

The whole publishing system was subject to the principles of strict centralism. The system, with its hierarchy of numerous levels, was unwieldy, bureaucratic and, therefore, excessively sluggish in its workings. The functions of the publishing houses were centralised to the hilt: all decisions concerning their creative, economic and production activities had to be referred to the powers above, who then issued instructions either permitting or forbidding proposed activities. Without approval from the *Goskomizdat*, publishing houses could not independently increase, if suddenly such a need arose, the size of a book by even one printer's sheet. Publishing houses, accustomed for decades to obeying and carrying out instructions, were surrounded on all sides by protective shields of all nature of strictly binding decisions and agreements, reviews and reglamentations. The purpose of this whole cumbersome bureaucratic publishing mechanism was to protect oneself against the need to take any risks or make any sort of independent decisions.

The bureaucratic administration of publishing is not merely something of recent times; it is a world-wide phenomenon with centuries-old traditions. Let us recall how many famous writers of the world personally suffered from its brutal attacks: Balzac, Jack London, Dostoevsky – tens, hundreds of names! Who will take the trouble to count the days, months, years lost by them in exhausting battle with publishers? For the sake of truth, let us admit that Soviet publishing added many of its own features to traditional bureaucratic practices. The publishing process, straitjacketed by the need to secure approval or permission for publication in a vast number of instances, resulted in an enormously inefficient use of time in the publishing of a book: from three to five years. Readers' opinion was never taken into consideration. They could in no way influence choices made concerning subject matter and the number of copies printed of each book, that is the main questions: what to publish and in what quantity. The role of the most important figure in the publishing business, the editor, was also severely diminished to the traditional one of stylist and proof-reader. His influence on the choice of writer and the subject of the book was virtually pared back to a minimum. All of this led inevitably to the castration of the activities of the publishing enterprises and their creative endeavours, and taught those in the profession to accustom themselves to living by a regime in which orders came from above and were unquestioningly executed. Unthinking obedience in the publishing business was the main source of the dull and second-rate books that often found no readers and filled the display windows of bookshops. That is how over many years book publishing became detached from the demands in real life.

The complex and cumbersome publishing system, which it was necessary to master from the very outset, provoked antagonism, a desire to tear asunder the chains of the regulations, directives and production norms with which the publishers were tightly bound hand and foot. In order to change this mechanism it had to be understood: what was essential to it and what had been imposed by the bureaucratic system? The eternal triangle in publishing of the author, publisher and reader created a system of complex relations.

It is beyond doubt that the conditions imposed by the Party's hegemony and the administrative apparatus added specific features to this complex relationship between the author and publisher. The section in the CC's Propaganda Department concerned with publishing houses and printing presses spent a substantial amount of its time controlling publishing enterprises and was at the same time over-burdened performing advocatory duties for extremely determined authors. Furthermore, it rendered support to writers who had submitted entirely second-rate manuscripts but were well apprised of where to turn and insistent in demanding the publication of their works. As a result of this practice, which was an example of Party patronage, a considerable quantity of poor literature was put out.

Conversations and meetings with publishers, printers and employees in the book trade showed that in Soviet book publishing a large number of critical problems had accumulated which needed solving. They could not be solved all at once; therefore, it was necessary to identify the most important ones, to prioritise. Towards these goals the devising of a special programme of action proved effective. The organisational base for this approach was special analysis groups which included the most highly qualified members of the *Goskomizdat*, academics from institutes, specialists from publishing companies, printing enterprises and book trading establishments. Five research groups were created. After completing a detailed analysis of the situation, their task was to present far-reaching proposals for the restructuring of the whole publishing business in Russia which would address such key issues as the democratisation of the organisational and creative activities of publishing houses, the perfection of printing processes, the development of the book trade, and the setting up of a system for investigating readers' wishes. A special group of analysts worked on questions concerning major changes to the administrative structure of publishing.

After a detailed examination of these proposals in each publishing, printing and book trade enterprise, a whole series of round tables and heated discussions with the heads of publishing houses, we deemed it possible to accept them as special resolutions. At the end of 1986 these resolutions were considered and approved at a session of the *Goskomizdat*, and in this way the guidelines for perestroika in the publishing business were set.

One of the first resolutions aimed at developing the creative initiative of publishing houses was 'On the broadening of the rights and independence of publishing houses', which was adopted in November 1986. In this resolution it was stated for the first time that the existing system of management and excessive regulation by the *Goskomizdat* and its daughter committees in the republics were seriously hindering the initiative, enterprise and independence of publishing houses. It also granted publishing houses the right to elaborate and adopt thematic projects, implement changes, publish different books and authors from in the past, and decide independently how many copies to publish of a given title.

On what does settling into a new profession depend? What above all helps one to establish oneself in a new job? I think it depends on the usefulness of one's new work and, of course, the interest which this work awakens in one. Together with experience from life comes understanding: neither duty nor one's position can replace the interest which the actual work should spark in one. I recall that at one of my meetings with readers at the Ostankino Television Studios I drew on Chekhov's short story *Darling* to illustrate the same point. Tolstoy had a very high opinion of this work and its main character. I do not think this was an arbitrary judgement: Tolstoy saw in the female character those extraordinary human virtues which are not always understood. Usually the leading character in Chekhov's story is interpreted ironically; however, after some reflection one discovers in this character the finest qualities of the human soul – devotion and self-sacrifice. It was not a conscious attempt to adapt to new circumstances which inspired Chekhov's *Darling* but a natural human evolution; when one's activities and personal attachments change, one develops new concerns, and with each day these duties take over one's thoughts, become dear to one and inseparable from one's life.

The changes which the times, with their ideas of democratisation, brought to the publishing houses, no matter how justified they were, did not arrive without causing some upset (as do all new measures); for they destroyed the old ways, did away with the bureaucratic system which people had grown accustomed to in publishing. I considered the most important element of these reforms to be granting publishing houses the freedom to make decisions, the right to choose who to publish and in how many copies. In order to frustrate any attempts at propping up the existing administrative system, in our resolution on the democratisation of the publishing business we consciously specified concomitant measures, such as the renunciation of the Committee's former compulsory censorship of manuscripts (which was given over entirely to the discretion of each publishing house), and in particular the ruling out of any form of covert censorship.

On the road to independence, of no small importance was releasing the creative energies of the editor – the main actor in the publishing process – from his bureaucratic shackles. To this end, a separate resolution of the *Goskomizdat* was adopted 'On the broadening of the rights and independence of editors of publishing houses', in which we attempted to define the primacy of editors in the selection of authors and subject area, and the editing of manuscripts. We wanted the editor to enjoy full rights in his direction of the publishing of a book, to the extent that he could take total personal responsibility for it.

I understand that my account of these reforms might seem boring or tedious to the average reader; however, for the publishing business at that time they signified a radical turning-point. They were valuable in that they made publishing houses receptive to everything in the real world with its new ideas and new authors.

It was clear to me that realisation of these measures would mean in practice the suicide of the *Goskomizdat*: the more independence the publishing enterprises acquired, the more superfluous the *Goskomizdat* would become. The Committee's basic functions would remain conducting surveys of readership demands and elaborating the government's publishing policy based on their findings.

Time subjects all our good intentions and plans, no matter what their nature, to pitiless examination. Though six years have passed since then, I still support the goal we set of defending Russian and Soviet literature and making it the property of every family. An unlimited project for publishing Russian and Soviet classics, unprecedented in the country's publishing history, was devoted to the realisation of this goal. First of all, in 1986, a three-volume publication of the works of Pushkin was published in the enormous number of 10,700,000 copies and was opened to unrestricted subscription. [Because sought-after books were mostly in short supply, a subscription system was set up whereby interested buyers could put their names down and pay the price of one volume for books before they were published and went on sale in bookshops. The subscription was often restricted to employees of certain establishments. – tr.] In 1987, a single-volume edition of Mayakovsky was issued in 6 million copies. In 1988, unrestricted subscription was conducted for the two-volume publication of Lermontov's works; its 14 million copies constituted a record number in both Soviet and international publishing. I cannot rule out, given today's inclination to reject everything, the possibility of criticisms emerging that this project was forced upon the publishing houses and that all other projects were subordinated to the narrow aims connected with the publication of Russian and Soviet classics. It is obvious that there are some grounds for such accusations. However, the fact that the policy would enable millions of families unrestrictedly to place these priceless treasures of our literature in their personal libraries fully vindicated our efforts.

Understanding that publishing policy should be finely tuned to the times and keep pace with them, in 1987 we drew up a publishing project known as 'fast reaction'. This programme undertook to publish fiction and journalistic works which had provoked a particularly broad public response immediately after they appeared in magazines. These books were issued in large quantities: no less than 200,000 copies within three-four months subsequent to their publication in magazines, rather than two or three years later, as used to be the case. After the project was launched, large number of copies were quickly published of the following works: *The Executioner's Block* by Chingis Aitmatov, V. Bykov's short story *The Sign of Misfortune*, V. Astafiev's novel *The Sad Detective*, D. Granin's novel *The Bison* and many other books by contemporary writers who had aroused especial interest. In 1987-88 as part of this series, little known or previously unpublished works by Akhmatova, Tsvetayeva, Bulgakov, Tvardovsky, Platonov, Nabokov, Grossman, Pasternak, and new works by Dudintsev, Rybakov and Pristavkin were published in very large numbers of copies.

We assessed our efforts objectively and viewed them as the beginning of the emancipation of publishing from administrative subjugation. The initial steps inspired optimism, for after gaining independence and as early as 1988 the publishing houses had struck from their publishing plans many books for which there was doubtful demand. This freed up material resources which enabled publishing houses to begin issuing books on the most topical social problems connected with perestroika. It was at that time that collected works by popular and well-known journalists were published: *No Other Choice* by Progress Publishers, *If According To One's Conscience* by the Sovetsky Pisatel publishing house, and *It Depends On Us (Perestroika in the Mirror of the Press)* by Knizhnaya Palata Publishers.

One consequence of the democratisation of the publishing business was the first attempts to repay the debt owed to its readers, starting with the publication of those authors whose works had long formed 'blank spaces' in the spiritual life of the country. Among the names restored were not only the writers whom I have already mentioned but also names of famous Russian philosophers and social activists: A. Losev, E. Radlov, N. Berdyaev, A. Chayanov, A. Vavilov, N. Bukharin, G. Zinoviev, L. Kamenev and L. Trotsky. Enormous interest in the forgotten pages of Russian and Soviet history was generated by the subscription and publication in large numbers of copies of multi-volume works of the historians Karamzin, Kostomarov, Klyuchevsky and Soloviev.

What helped me to overcome the resistance I encountered and believe in the success of the reforms? Above all the fact that I had seen that interest had been revived in people in independent work free of supervision and pressures from above. By 1988 publishing's centre of gravity was increasingly moving from the *Goskomizdat* directly to the publishing houses and printing offices. People in our country have long ceased to believe in the altruism of directives from the top authorities and suspect those who determine the measures of certain vested interests. There certainly were interests, but they were aimed at nothing more sinister than the destruction of bureaucratism in publishing and freeing it from meddling by the powers above.

A Sense of Futility: The Commercialisation of Publishing

Publishing – the most vital sector of our country's culture – was going through a time of contradictions. This was manifested in the fact that, on the one hand, positive changes were taking place: creative and economic independence became the norm for the majority of publishing houses. Many of the administrative rules and prohibitions disappeared. The reader could now freely purchase books by writers and scholars whose works had, for a long time, been banned. The appearance, alongside state publishing houses, of alternative commercial ones created a fundamentally new situation in the book world, the essence of which consisted in the destruction of the state monopoly of publishing and the appearance of real competition between state and commercial publishing houses. The first steps taken by the latter already showed that they respond more actively to the demands of the market and thus force state publishing houses to speed up their output. This phenomenon caused a fundamental change in the whole state of the book market.

During the establishment of market relations, however, negative features also clearly manifested themselves, putting state publishing in the difficult position of trying to survive. The main one was the commercialisation of publishing, which led to a sharp fall in the output of socially necessary literature: children's, textbook, scientific and technological – that is, that which ensured the existence of society's intellectual potential.

This is how the situation took shape in publishing in this country during the change in its volume and structure. the peak of book production was reached in 1988: 2 billion 700 million books. In subsequent years, as might have been expected under the conditions of the broad development in the number of commercial publishing houses and given the limited capacity of the country's printing and paper production facilities, the number of books produced in state publishing houses began to fall. Over the two years from 1989 to 1990, book production here fell by more than 700 million copies. It should be noted that similar drops in book production only occurred twice in the history of the USSR: in 1937 and 1941-1942. Of course, not only the significant fall in the volume of state book production caused concern. There was a drop in the output of literature particularly required by society, including, above all, children's, the output of which fell by almost 250 million copies over these two years in question. In 1990 alone, the output of children's editions dropped by 33%, that of textbooks by 15% and that of scientific and technological literature by 14%. There was, at the same time, a marked reduction in state publishing houses in the volume of fiction and socio-political literature produced, the number of copies falling by 6% and 19% respectively in a year. In 1991, the trend towards a further drop in the volume of book production gained impetus and, in 1992, in connection with the beginning of the economic reform and introduction of free prices, became catastrophic: the 20-fold rise in paper prices made publishing generally unprofitable. According to the Ministry of Publications and Information of Russia, there was a 40% drop in book production during the first half of 1992.

During these years, the loss of state publishing houses was to some degree replenished by commercial ones. Of the four thousand registered publishing houses in 1992, about half were either private firms or publishing houses with mixed forms of ownership. By 1990 the number of books produced by non-state publishing houses had increased six-fold since 1988 and constituted about 8% of the total number of books published in the country. There was a particular rise in the amount of fiction published by commercial publishing houses and, according to certain data, by 1991 constituted more than 20% of the total. In the first half of 1992, one in four books was published by a non-state publishing house, and among fiction and children's literature – one in three.

The transition to free prices and competition with commercial publishing houses had, by 1992, put state publishing houses in an extremely difficult position in obtaining paper and persuading printing works to accept their orders. Owing to various government financial regulations, state publishing houses were not on an equal footing with joint and small ventures engaged in publishing. Commercial publishing houses often purchased paper and paid for printing in cash, at prices beyond those which the state could pay. As a result, it was more profitable for both state-owned and commercial printing and paper combines to deal with commercial publishing houses.

However paradoxical it might seem, the democratic changes with the introduction of market mechanisms have also, at the current stage, brought publishing to a destruction of social links. The experience of 1992 has shown that the establishment of market relations in publishing have led to the loss of the main social orientation, for the tremendous (20-30-fold) rise in outlays on paper, printing services and the sale of editions have compelled publishers to raise book prices unprecedentedly and thus restrict access to them for broad social circles of potential readers.

The multiple rise in the cost of books alongside the growth in prices for all other goods has resulted in the rating of consumer interest and, correspondingly, the demand for books, falling among the list of essential commodities. The year 1992 was quite unique in that, for the first time in a decade, there was no longer a shortage of books, in spite of the drop in the overall number of books published, particularly children's, textbooks and scientific ones. In contrast to the recent past, books were no longer among the consumers' priorities and became simply inaccessible for millions of ordinary people. I am greatly alarmed by and sincerely regret the alienation of the broad population from books, which means from culture in general. The market has put mass popular periodicals and books virtually beyond the reach of the majority of the population, living on the verge of poverty. These include 50 million pensioners, 30 million invalids and disabled people, and 40 million schoolchildren and students.

The inaccessibility of books for millions of real and potential readers is exacerbated by the extreme impoverishment of public libraries, which are virtually without funds for purchasing books. According to sociological research in April 1992 by Professor B. Grushin's service for social opinion surveys, more than half the population did not look at a book in the course of the month and are no longer considered readers, while 21% had not opened a book for a year. In this respect, reading constitutes one of the most sensitive indicators of the state of society.

With respect to the above research, the question undoubtedly arises as to what and whom people do read today. Among the six most popular genres, detective novels, science fiction and adventure stories came in first place, followed by foreign classics, then modern fiction, with historical novels in fourth place, Russian classics in fifth and books by Russian emigrés in sixth. The most read book in Russia was Margaret Mitchell's *Gone with the Wind*. This fact appears quite significant, reflecting the current state of readers' interests. Among Russian authors, Valentin Pikul, who writes adventure stories based on Russian history, retained his first place. Among romantic adventures, the best read still include the Golons' numerous Angelique novels, Burrows' Tarzan books, the well-known classic detective novels by Chase and Christie, and the immortal Dumas novels.

Foreign classical authors were ranked as follows: Charlotte Brontë, Dreiser, Remarque, Druon, Maupassant, Maurois and Dickens. The Soviet writers mentioned included Rybakov, Grossman, Aitmatov, Bondarev, Karpov, Anatoli Ivanov. The leader among Russian classic writers was Dostoyevsky, the interest in his works being particularly great owing to the numerous former bans, his *The Possessed* having been published for a broad readership only two years ago. Then follow Gogol, Turgenev, Chekhov, Mamin-Sibiryak and Gorky. Among Russian books written abroad, first place belongs to Solzhenitsyn's *Gulag Archipelago*, followed by the works of Nabokov, Bunin and Brodsky.

There is currently a certain boom in memoirs, foremost among which are the previously prohibited reminiscences of prerevolutionary and postrevolutionary activists: Savinkov, Denikin, Milyukov, Shulgin and Khrushchev. Memoirs by women have also attracted attention: Vishnevskaya, Vladi, Alliluyeva, Bukharina and Gorbacheva.

However we may condemn the shortcomings of Soviet society as a whole, however much we may criticise it for its strict administrative centralism, we cannot but admit that there were inherent in it regulations that were basically humanitarian. These included the traditionally low prices for books, the purpose having been to ensure that each family could acquire the minimum necessary number of books. In commercial respects, this publishing policy, in contrast to generally adopted international practice, put the publication of children's, textbooks, many types of scientific, technological and narrowly professional literature in a difficult position. In its social orientation, however, it was justified, especially considering that the average wage enjoyed by the majority of the working population meant that no other publishing policy was possible.

What is the way out of the current critical situation? How can state publishing be protected during these complex times? I believe that now is the time to do, at last, what many publishing houses have been asking for many years. Considering the tremendous social and national significance of book publishing in the protection and development of the country's culture, the state, the President of Russia and the Government should reject the long-term policy of receiving any profit from book publication. In contrast to a consumption policy, one of state and social protectionism should be pursued towards the country's publishing. The first step towards this was the Russian Presidential Decree of February 1992 in defence of publishing, which listed measures for protecting children's and textbook literature. Unfortunately, these measures have not been implemented.

What does a policy of state protectionism mean? It must be based on an optimal tax model, rejecting administrative forms of plunderous taxation and a transition to progressive taxation, i.e., differentiated taxes depending on the type of publication, its social significance and technical complexity. No matter how difficult Russia's current financial situation, it would already be fair to exempt from all taxes the publication of children's, textbook, and scientific literature and books of classical fiction, as well as books by Russian authors, so that they might sell abroad. These proposals contain nothing new or unusual. Worldwide publishing practice includes the real and long-established existence in many countries of differentiated taxes on book publishing (from 6% to 12% of the total profits), while certain types of literature – children's, textbooks, export – are totally exempt from state taxes.

Four well-known Academicians of the Russian Academy of Sciences, Leonid Leonov, Dmitri Likhachev, Guri Marchuk and Igor Sokolov-Petryanov, have written a bitter open letter to the parliaments and governments of the countries of the CIS in the newspaper *Kultura* (October 13, 1992), concerning the collapse of publishing, the unprecedentedly high cost of books and the significant drop, by almost 50%, in the literature the people need, especially children's, classical fiction and scientific and technological books. 'The pain we feel for books, for the currently demeaned position,' they note, 'compels us to raise our voices in their defence.' They ask that urgent state measures be taken to save book publishing, which constitutes the material foundation of the country's science and culture. Their proposals include a change in the taxation system, the introduction of preferential tariffs for the transportation and postage of books. The Academicians' letter is a serious argument in favour of a policy of state protectionism towards publishing.

I would like to note that protectionism does not mean just state patronage. A special place in a system of protectionism may belong to the actual book purchasers from among the number of interested public, scientific, production and commercial organisations and individual patrons interested in financing loss-making publications that are necessary for the development of national culture and science.

Chapter 5 - A Chance Missed:
In the USSR Committee for
Television and Radio

Television came into my life like an express train arriving with a clatter of wheels at a small station, filling it with the hustle and bustle of a crowd of fussy passengers, and stirring up a somnolent little town.

In a similar fashion, events that led to my appointment unfolded remarkably rapidly, which in itself was quite unusual. During a break in the April 1989 plenary session of the Central Committee of the Communist Party Mikhail Gorbachev talked with me about routine matters and finally, as if in passing, said that he wanted to discuss a serious question. I thought little about that at the time and just waited for him to get in touch with me. Several days later, in early May, V.A. Medvedev, the then Central Committee Secretary, asked me to come to his office. He said: 'We [more often than not, the plural was used in the Central Committee for expressing the opinion of only one person] know that you have many quite productive plans for the publishing industry and a lot of work to do in order to carry them out. However, it is imperative that we urgently strengthen the leadership of the USSR State Committee for Television and Radio. It has been suggested that you be appointed to the Committee.'

V.A. Medvedev and I were on an informal footing because we had earlier worked as equals in the propaganda section of the Central Committee of the Communist Party. That is why I could be perfectly frank with him. I said I did not know the workings of television and, for that matter, had no taste for it and did not see any sense in being moved from one job to another, since publishing was also important in shaping public opinion. I told him in so many words that the Central Committee expected a new head of the main body for television and radio to do the impossible: mollify political passions mounting in television and radio broadcasts and bring about an immediate change. I did not delude myself into thinking that someone could pour oil on troubled waters. Passions were not stirred up by the Ostankino studios but by rather life itself. I tried to open the eyes of the April Plenum to this truth. Participants in that plenum were verbally tearing strips off the Chairman of the Committee for Television and Radio for a television show in which Mark Zakharov for the first time ever spoke in front of a nationwide audience about removing Lenin's body from the Mausoleum in the Kremlin. A.N. Aksenov, the then television head, weakly tried to explain that it had been merely an isolated incident and promised to look into it and take appropriate measures. I felt very sorry for Aksenov; I had worked for quite a while in the mass media and knew the situation too well not to recognise that by 1989 it was no longer possible to satisfy the Central Committee's demand that passions be toned down and journalists be kept in check.

I do not know whether Medvedev stood up for me, but not a full week later Gorbachev called me on the telephone to say that he would shortly go to the People's Republic of China on an official visit and had planned to meet with me when he returned, but the matter brooked no delay, so he wanted to return to the conversation which Medvedev had had with me on his behalf. I told him that although we had already discussed everything, I wanted to repeat my request not to be transferred because I was involved in a very useful business and furthermore I did not believe in a quick fix for television. Gorbachev's response was categorical: 'The situation with television is difficult; it requires fresh approaches and new people. The Politburo members are of one mind that none other than you should take that position. It is decided.' I stood my ground and again asked that a different decision be found. Gorbachev said: 'All right, I see what you think about it, but I am also asking you to agree to this job. I am not insisting but just asking you to consider the present situation and agree.'

On May 17, 1989, the Praesidium of the USSR Supreme Soviet issued a decree on my appointment as Chairman of the USSR State Committee for Television and Radio (Gosteleradio). This opened a new, short and the most dramatic page in my life.

The Unfathomable World of Television

The three years I spent in the television business were the busiest of all. I was snowed under with work and big and small challenges of every nature. In some ways they were similar to those I faced working for *Sovetskaya Rossiya*, yet their scale was far greater. True, in contrast with the newspaper, from the very beginning I became conscious that the returns from my daily nervous strain and unsparing efforts were amazingly low. That was why I was constantly plagued by a feeling of helplessness in trying to radically change something in the operation of this huge information monster.

I took me some time to understand much of what I am mentioning in this book. At that time I still entertained a hope and sincerely believed in the success of the reforms known as perestroika, which were expected to bring about marked changes in Gosteleradio.

Everybody has his own notion about television. Mine was basically that television was not only a world all of its own and a special form of creativity but it also meant distinctive relationships between people who were involved in an intricate process of the integration of various media: information, cinematography, drama and music which influenced the minds and emotions of a huge audience. Since this complex world is open to many interpretations everybody has a right to his own opinion on what television is and what it is not, and may demand from it what is consonant with his interests, while rejecting or ignoring much of what it means for others.

What then did I see and understand in this huge and bewildering world of television; what was I prepared to accept and what went counter to my convictions? What was my television like?

Television is a beloved and cruel child of leaders and their nation and a source of their joys and sorrows. It is not only a pampered child in the mass media family but also a late one and, like all late children, it has not only unquestionable virtues but also unavoidable deficiencies and shortcomings. While it was one of the most powerful means of communication with wide reach and influence, far less qualified journalists and editors were employed on television than in other news media, including the press, where more expertise had been amassed. It could easily be seen that those people who held leading positions in the music, art education and feature film sections in television studios were anything but leading specialists in drama, motion pictures and music. I think this had much to do with the special attraction of television at the initial stage of its development, when it was the 'in' thing and attracted all those who had failed to make the grade in other forms of mass media and now tried to establish themselves in television. It is probably for this reason that a considerable number of semi-professionals, Jacks-of-all-trades but masters of none, have held down jobs in the television business.

I never made a secret of not being an ardent fan of television and have always regarded it as a rather superficial form of mass media, largely based on improvisation and visual images, 'pictures', with little substance. The printed word is closer to me, because I have always marvelled at how words one writes on a blank sheet of paper can convey a whole range of thought and exciting ideas that provoke an emotional response in one. Whether or not my partiality is justified, I have high regard for the printed word and I feel that it is more weighty, honest and sincere because no one is able to disclaim the printed word.

I came to realise that television had an awesome potential and could profoundly influence society in many ways – stir up the whole country, foment unrest, cause wide-scale destruction and human tragedies – due to its powerful synthesis of the spoken word, visual images and the emotional impact of drama and music. On the other hand, it could direct the thoughts of the people to vital issues, make them concerned for the destiny of their country, console them at times of tribulation and misery, impart wisdom and inspire them with kindness and mercy.

In order to comprehend the phenomenon of television I proceeded from an understanding that it was an integral and inalienable part of everyday life, as it did not develop and change in and of itself but only through the direct influence of the changes under way in society. Complain as we may about it, there is no arguing that television cannot be any better than life itself. No matter how vehemently we condemn television for its non-objectivity and partiality, it merely mirrors life in all of its aspects, more faithfully reflecting life as it is, good and evil, sorrows and joys than any of the other mass media. Despite criticism that there were too many errors and absurdities in our broadcasts I always found consolation in that there was a great deal more idiocy and absurdity in 'real' life. At countless government and public meetings where we were told that we ought to be ashamed of showing the ugly underside of our life I could not help but ask: 'aren't you yourselves ashamed of living so disgracefully, working so badly and governing the country so unwisely?'

In my view, that television mirrored real life and could not be any better than what it reflected by no means meant that its function was confined only to that of a mirror. Today, in a country of openness and freedom of information, like any of the mass media television is not merely a mirror but is shaping public opinion more and more, exerting strong and frequently direct influence on people's minds. True enough, television cannot be better than life itself, but beyond doubt it should not seek to make it worse than it is. If television is essentially what life is then it is equally true that life is similar to the way television shows it. The more people who heap accusations on others appear on the television screen and the more destructive talk is heard on the air, the closer society is pushed towards spiritual collapse and anarchy. I think that the well-known injunction concerning the moral conduct of a physician − 'thou shalt not do any harm' − is just as relevant for television professionals as it is for doctors, because they hold in their hands a very powerful tool: public opinion.

As it could be expected, television, the most influential form of news media, was at the cutting edge of the social reforms launched in 1985 and became one of the main vehicles of perestroika. On the other hand, the impact of changes occurring in society on television became greater by the day, making it more open and critical. Its dialogues on burning economic, political and cultural issues captured a huge audience of viewers while television was under increasing pressure from a whole range of opinions from all sectors of society.

Far be it from me to accuse my predecessors in Gosteleradio of completely ignoring viewers' interests. As is known, back in the 1970s the USSR Committee for Television and Radio was among the first of the mass media to set up a service for surveying public opinion on television broadcasts and programming. Established for this purpose were the Main Editorial Offices for Letters and Sociological Surveys. Every year Central Television received over 500,000 letters which were read and analysed; in addition, regular polls were taken to monitor shifts in viewers' opinions about individual programmes. Of course, the survey service was not perfect and could not instantly provide us with data for the assessment of shows' ratings. Nonetheless, its assessment of major trends in the interest and attitudes of the radio and television audience was accurate. Surveys and the day-to-day operation of television and radio showed that in the previous years, in circumstances where political struggle steadily mounted in the Soviet Union, the mass audience had been least satisfied with information programmes which they regarded as inaccurate and openly partisan and non-objective in the coverage of events.

It is well known that heated debates on information and its interpretation and assessment by the news media, as well as what is and what is not a permissible extent of a journalist's and show presenter's personal treatment of the contents of information programmes, have been going on for a long time. Widely differing opinions have been voiced. However, it was obvious at the time that under the policy of glasnost and increasing openness a dramatic change had occurred in this country. A great leap had been made from one extreme – 'talking heads' straightjacketed by strict rules mechanically reading official texts which had to be approved by countless senior bureaucrats – to the other where it was virtually mandatory for presenters to comment on and interpret all events. In a situation aggravated by confrontation between various political forces and acute social and ethnic conflicts, which had in many cases grown into all-out wars, subjective assessments by radio and television presenters incite protests and ultimatums, quite frequently fuelling confrontation. For instance, if a presenter of *Vesti*, a news programme on a countrywide television channel, says that according to unspecified sources the troops of the 14th Army move towards Kishinev, it means in practice that rumours are treated as newsworthy and are given much play by one of the government television channels. As a result the rumour turns into misinformation and, consequently, provocation.

Many foreign colleagues I have met were scandalised by this

phenomenon, widespread in this country, and the extreme and unjustified personal treatment of the contents of news broadcasts by journalists and programme presenters. S. Muratov noted in an *Izvestia* article for October 3, 1992: while in the past foreigners were shocked by the extremely official tone and contents of the programme *Vremya*, today they are surprised by our journalists' presumptuous belief that their opinions about facts are more relevant than the facts themselves. Television journalists have come to believe that they are missionaries rather than news presenters.

On business trips abroad I have had an opportunity to familiarise myself with strict rules that are binding for leading Western television companies. The majority of them have officially laid down ethical codes which employees pledge to follow when signing their contracts. These codes specifically emphasise that broadcasters should never presume that their interests and personal views, as well as those of the social groups they belong to, represent the whole range of opinion in their countries. Some of these codes contain dire warnings concerning the observance of one binding rule or another in reporting news on television. For example, the NBC News house code of ethics cautions that unverified rumours may lead to a disaster; information from outside sources should not be included in programmes unless it is confirmed by the police, an NBC corespondent on location or other recognised authorities or sources.

A large section of television viewers in the middle and senior age groups, in the Russian provinces, Central Asia and the Caucasus were especially irritated by the dominance of rock music in programming, which squeezed out ethnic music, and countless groups of extremely eccentric-looking and unprofessional performers playing music in a wild and objectionable manner, who had invaded television. Central Television production teams and programme presenters were accused in numerous letters from viewers, as well as at USSR Supreme Soviet sessions and in parliamentary committees, of promoting group interests and non-objectivity. Authors of programmes featuring only issues relevant for Moscow and Leningrad alone were harshly criticised for the narrowness of subjects. For a very good reason, many people maintained that there was a glaring discrepancy between the name of

Central, i.e. country-wide, Television and the contents of its programming, which represented only Moscow.

I was aware of many of these shortcomings; so this was no revelation for me. As a television viewer I had recognised that all was not rosy in the garden even before I stopped being an outsider, and for the most part I saw the criticism as sober and justified. However, at the time I knew little about the sources of the problems besetting television and the antagonism, as it were, between Central Television and its audience.

Understanding the intricate workings and special features of television as a business and forming my own position were not an educational but a very practical objective for me, as I had to determine if it was possible to direct this powerful information mechanism and to what extent it was amenable to management. Central Television went on the air from Moscow at that time on four channels. Considering the fact that the first and second channels broadcast programmes more than once for various time zones in order to make up for the time difference, Central Television was on the air for a total of 160 hours per day. In addition, a network of 122 independent regional television centres operated around the country. Radio broadcasts were also beamed from Moscow and 176 regional stations. Besides that, international broadcasts from Radio Moscow in 66 languages could be picked up in 160 countries around the world.

Management in television and radio was subject to the same principles of a command-and-administrative system as all the other government-run structures under the guidance of the CPSU Central Committee. As far as its financial and material potential was concerned, Gosteleradio was fully dependent on the Council of Ministers. That is why the Committee's Chairman acted as a member of the Government. In the creative domain and in the shaping of the policy of radio and television broadcasting the work of this organisation was directly controlled by the Central Committee of the Communist Party. Therefore it was mandatory for the Gosteleradio Chairman to be on hand for sessions of the Secretariat and Politburo of the CPSU Central Committee at which broadcasts were assessed and instructions handed down concerning the most important information reports and speeches. Since I had taken part in sessions of the Secretariat of the CPSU Central Committee for eight years in my capacity as the Editor-in-Chief of the *Sovetskaya Rossiya* I had had ample opportunity to observe the response of CC secretaries to specific programmes and knew well the criticism leveled at virtually each session at the then Gosteleradio Chairman, S.G. Lapin, and his successor, A.N. Aksenov.

The CC Secretariat and Politburo were generally ill-disposed towards the heads of Gosteleradio. This negative attitude could be explained by the fact that for all the gloss and veneer, television nonetheless impartially mirrored events and those who made them. It pitilessly exposed the mediocrity and ineptitude of the leaders before the whole nation. Perhaps no person and news media conveyed such unvarnished truth about the real worth of this country's leaders – Brezhnev and Chernenko – as television. The harder the propaganda machine tried to boost their images as leaders of genius the clearer television reflected their physical and mental inadequacy.

I well remember that at one session of the Secretariat M.A. Suslov very critically remarked to S.G. Lapin that the latter gave insufficient air time to the Central Committee leaders and members of the Government. Lapin was astute and experienced enough not to enter into an argument and took that caustic remark with an air of humble respect. However, he later said with ironic annoyance to L. Tolkunov, who had also taken part in the Secretariat meeting, and myself that the CC owed him gratitude for not showing those who ruled the country for what they really were, for millions of viewers to see.

The years I spent working in the USSR State Committee for Television and Radio coincided with the time when perestroika began running out of steam. There was growing dissatisfaction among wide sections of the population with the course of reforms. No matter what and how much was said at the time about the insidiousness of the opposition, this process in effect boosted the popularity of and support for the democratic opposition to Mikhail Gorbachev's policies. The number of mass media professionals who joined the opposition at that point was quite substantial. This, as could be expected, stirred up severe criticism of radio and television across the political spectrum. In *Literaturnaya Rossiya* articles, television was condemned as a source of extreme free-thinking, a vehicle for the destruction of the spiritual foundations of society and its values, and accused of spreading immorality; the magazine *Ogonyok* fired broadsides at television, claiming that it remained as conservative as in the past, was out of step with the press in freedom of thought and failed to reflect the pluralism of modern society.

Television and its boss came in for especially scathing criticism for dissidence from the leaders of the CPSU Central Committee and the Government, who frequently demonstrated an amazing lack of understanding of what was in reality happening in this country. I concluded from continuous debates at meetings convened to discuss some specific shows and the arguments put forward at these meetings that the old idea that the real problem lay in who should and who should not be allowed to speak into the microphones on radio and television persisted in the Gorbachev closest circle. The matter was not only that their approach was a shortsighted and unprofessional one but, what was more important, that they were quite used to running television by decrees and were blind to what went on outside their offices in Old Square and the Kremlin.

Criticism from above was so severe and unsparing that on some occasions it put one in mind of the ancient practice of beheading a messenger who brought bad news to the palace of a ruler. It never occurred to those who meted out such summary justice that the messenger could not be blamed for whatever went wrong but was in fact himself a victim of the news it was his duty to report. I am speaking about it with bitterness because I was convinced that television and radio must not have two levels of truth and openness. For example, one level was for the live coverage of a congress of People's Deputies or a Supreme Soviet session, where passions were high and opinions clashed and brimmed over with no regard for even the basic rules of conduct and courtesy. Television brought the ugly scenes to the homes of millions of viewers. Then on the day after it was strange to hear Gorbachev's statements and indignant remarks made on his behalf about the programme hosts and observers who had too openly or too caustically commented on the clashes between the parliament members. Hearing these statements, I wondered how they found it possible to shift gear to a completely different level of openness on the following day by order of the top leaders given the extremely tense political situation. Only by an enormous stretch of the imagination could this over-heated atmosphere of a Congress of People's Deputies of the Soviet Union or the Russian Federation be presented in radio and television commentaries as a peaceful, businesslike and sober one. Every fiery word and feeling to which the deputies, rivals in a race for power, gave expression from the congress rostrum was immediately given much play in interviews, commentaries and discussions by journalists.

The widespread political fever of the late 1980s hideously distorted the atmosphere on countrywide radio and television and deformed their workings. Following the start of the First Congress of People's Deputies in May 1989, every congress session was broadcast nationwide – live from beginning to end – upon the insistent demand of the deputies. Millions of people were riveted to their television sets all day long. There was no time left for working, as virtually the whole adult population in every corner of the country was totally preoccupied with the political debates. The Palace of Congresses in the Kremlin turned into a theatre where the most tense and tragic stage play in the history of this country was performed; television was one of the key actors in that extravaganza. By the end of the congress it had become perfectly clear that television had started interfering with the normal work of the parliament. More and more, many of the debates resembled television shows where MPs only sought to draw attention to themselves. Half-way through the congress, after sharp disputes, it was decided to go on broadcasting the sessions in full but only late at night. This started nationwide night-long vigils in front of television sets. I well remember that at the Second Congress of the USSR People's Deputies in the Kremlin controversy concerning the Gdlian and Ivanov case lasted until midnight and then the broadcast of that session continued until 5 a.m. I came home from the Palace of Congresses at 1 a.m., switched on my TV set and sat for a long time, thinking about where these night-time debates would lead us. I had no idea of where we were going. Now I know.

My colleagues from Japanese, Finnish and US television companies, professionals whom I met at the time, would frequently comment about the innovations in our television, which amounted to an unprecedented interference with this country's political life. They told me frankly that it was important for them to study the unique phenomenon of the mass political psychosis which had not spared any sector of society and was being inflamed in a well-orchestrated and purposeful manner through the powerful media of radio and television. With undisguised irony they noted that the notorious experimental psychologists, Kashpirovsky and Chumak, had been squeezed out from programming by drawn-out broadcasts of month-long congress sessions and conferences of the top Communist Party and Soviet Government bodies, which lasted well into the night and usually did not end until 2 or 3 a.m. Foreign journalists openly voiced their doubts about these 'innovative experiments' by Soviet television. Many of them believed that a special laboratory should be set up in order to assess the extent of the influence of such broadcasts of major political and social events on people's minds. Western television specialists suggested that these experiments not only did little to bolster public trust and aggravated disappointment but also instilled confusion in people's minds, lack of confidence; against the sinister backdrop of a crumbling economy, decline in production, perennial supply shortages and growing impoverishment the 'innovations' annoyed viewers, the majority of whom would rather watch something else on television.

Thinking about the comments of my Western colleagues and my own role in this process, I fully realised that the criticism was justified, because it was an objective reflection of the deformed condition of Central Television, brought about by the general politicisation of all aspects of life. The only excuse I could find for myself was that such a state of affairs was a problem for television, though itself was not to blame, as it mirrored the deformations existing in a society politicised to the hilt. The deformation went so far that there was no room for literature, art and culture. I remember that in late May 1990 I came home earlier than usual and by force of habit, as I did in my office, skipped from one television channel to another. This is what I saw: a congress of People's Deputies was being shown on Channel Two; a session of the Moscow Municipal Council on Moscow Channel, and one of its Leningrad counterpart on the Leningrad channel; Channel One was broadcasting a report on a session of the USSR Supreme Soviet. As I watched these programmes I could well imagine what ideas an ordinary viewer might have formed about our television, and this upset me very much. Nor did the viewers only think but they also wrote poignantly desperate letters to the Committee for Television and Radio, in which they protested against our turning this country into a madhouse with the help of television. But the captive viewers, hostages to politicians, who had absolutely no say in the contents of programming, could do nothing to change this situation. What could they do about it if each of the first sessions of People's Deputies of the USSR and the Russian Federation opened with a unanimous – a sign of the time – decision 'on behalf of the whole nation' on the broadcasting of all sessions in full?

Going back to our recent past, I cannot help thinking that nothing goes unpunished. I believe that no one has contributed so much to the glorification and collapse of this country's parliament as television.

On many occasions in my conversations with Gorbachev, Ryzhkov and Lukyanov I brought up the issues I was most concerned about: the impotence and lack of rights of the Chairman of the State Committee for Television and Radio and the impossibility of putting an end to the negative changes in television by old command and administrative methods. My position was basically as follows: the practice of imposing all manner of old-style bans should be dropped in dealing with the editorial sections on television. In addition, it was necessary for us to try and gradually create an atmosphere where television and radio would represent all points of view on television, with no one political movement, party and organisation dominating and enjoying a monopoly. Given the political confrontation and the fluid and complex situation it entailed, in order to push through my views, two conditions were prerequisite as a minimum: the ability to exercise common sense and an understanding on the part of Gorbachev and his close circle. True, to make this possible, Gorbachev should have at least trusted in the integrity of the Gosteleradio Chairman both in that he was not a careerist and schemer and was no less concerned for the future of his country and people than Mr Gorbachev himself, and that he sought to put an end to the process of disintegration which had spread to every sector of society and affected every aspect of social life. I do not think Gorbachev was capable of doing so, as he trusted no one but himself. Even if this condition had been met, the second one would be just as important: one had to have the courage and will to convince others that they should not serve one leader or another but act according to the dictates of their conscience; one also needed to find the social forces and individuals capable of opposing the dominance of group interests and monopolism and to create a situation where television and radio could truly reflect the whole range of opinion.

Chairman of Gosteleradio

In a country where political passions and conflicts overwhelmed society and were expressed as open hostility in the struggle for power, the position of chairman of USSR Gosteleradio was difficult and contradictory. Nearly every day the head of television would end up in the centre of some kind of conflict and in the position of choosing between opposing forces where he invariably turned out to be wrong no matter what decision was made. I'm not going to shed tears in order to elicit sympathy, but I will say, as my grandmother used to, that the situation was such that I wouldn't have wished it on my worst enemy. Now when there is time to reflect and evaluate that difficult period of time from a distance, I confess that no matter how terrible it was, my own nature helped me to cope, my habit of not indulging in intrigues and deceits, not playing anyone's games, remaining true to my own self even in the most trying situations.

The conflict between Gorbachev and Yeltsin was one of the facts of public life in the late 1980s which turned out to have an enormous influence on the development of political events in this country. I'm convinced that no one, not even a great prophet, could have foreseen how fatal it would turn out to be for the fate of our Motherland. I think that even those of our journalists who more than anyone else fanned the flames of this conflict, would now have thought twice before spreading that destructive fire. It is clear that even Gorbachev, had he had the slightest inkling of the consequences of his conflict with the political dissident from Sverd-lovsk, would not have listened so closely to the conservatives from his inner circle and would have rejected the Communist Party's usual manner of dealing with dissident political rivals.

The distinctive quality of television was that, in the confront-ation between political antagonists, it could not remain neutral and unavoidably turned out to be either the immediate culprit in the outbreak of conflict or the scapegoat on which to place all blame. There were many examples of this. I will take only two of these which at the time had a large public impact. The first was connected with Boris Yeltsin's trip to the United States in 1989. Up to that time I had met Yeltsin only once. It was in autumn 1984 in Sverd-lovsk, where I arrived as editor-in-chief of the newspaper *Sovet-skaya Rossiya* to meet with our readers. There was a friendly atti-tude towards the paper in the Sverdlovsk regional party committee. The committee's propaganda secretary V. Zhitenev and the secre-tary of the city party committee A. Andrianov were known to me as energetic, motivated workers. In Sverdlovsk I had interesting meetings with readers in industrial enterprises, at the scientific cen-tre, and at the upper party school.

I learned from conversations with my colleagues in Sverdlovsk that their attitude to the first secretary of the regional party committee was respectful and friendly. They thought that the authority of the leading figure in the region was not merely a func-tion of the position, but was due to his qualities as a natural leader. I was told about the solidarity and friendliness of the regional com-mittee workers not only at work but also in volleyball competitions and in social evening get-togethers with families and colleagues.

Boris Yeltsin was one of the few first secretaries of regional party committees who tried to get rid of the customary formal ties and relations between a party leader and ordinary people and tried to meet and openly talk with different categories of working people including workers, scholars, and the intelligentsia. In *Sovetskaya Rossiya* we wrote at the time of hours-long meetings of Yeltsin with Sverdlovsk students at the Palace of Sports where he answered all questions, including the most difficult ones, frankly and openly without hiding anything. As a result of our first meeting and con-versation I formed a distinct personal impression of Boris Yeltsin.

I remember the conversation was about the lead article entitled *The Party Worker* written by me and published in the paper. As a representative of the party workaholics who were adherents of the strong-willed style, Boris Yeltsin thought that my thesis: 'Neither the number of working hours, nor a seven-day working week guarantee success, but erudition and a high degree of professionalism', was incorrect, for in conditions where so much depended on the party's intervention, there was no way, proceeding from rational methods, to economise on time. 'In Sverdlovsk,' he remarked to me, 'the party workers don't have set hours, we work however many hours the job requires without sparing either time or ourselves.' The finality of his judgements and his limited ability to understand his interlocutor as well as the timidity and silence of my fellow ideologues from Sverdlovsk who were present at the meeting showed that Yeltsin favoured direct open relations, but was one of those people who are born to command and make independent decisions. He did not appear to me to be a great democrat. Yeltsin was one of those party leaders who, not from any Samizdat pamphlet but through real experience in the 1970s, knew about the decay of the party system, its deformities from top to bottom, its immunity to change and inability to reform. On the other hand, he had already been formed by the party system as a leader and could not change the kind of person he was, someone who was disposed towards making decisions on his own and was not accustomed to listen to what other people think, to take advice, or to consider the opinions of people more knowledgeable than himself in any particular sphere of activity.

Yeltsin's move to Moscow and his rapid appointment to the post of secretary of the Moscow city party committee that followed shortly afterwards were met with interest and, I won't conceal it, approval by us at *Sovetskaya Rossiya*. To no small degree this was connected with the fact that the paper was embroiled in frequent conflicts with Victor Grishin who would not tolerate any criticism from the press relating to Moscow. I am writing about this in order to point out that I did not have any grounds for hostility towards Yeltsin although, I admit, I didn't see him as a radical democratic leader who was capable of bringing justice and good to our long-suffering people.

After Yeltsin's trip to the United States a reprint of an article from the Italian newspaper *Repubblica* appeared in *Pravda*. In this article Yeltsin was portrayed as an immoderate man who did not know how to conduct himself in decent society. This publication elicited various opinions and gossip and there were requests to show Yeltsin's appearances in the USA on Soviet television. People talked about why our television remained silent. Western journalists in Moscow offered us their own videotapes of Yeltsin's appearances. After discussing the matter with the deputies, we decided to show these tapes on Central Television.

I repeat here what I told journalists when they asked me about this scandalous story. I did not like the reprinted article in *Pravda* which was in the typical style of the tabloids with its familiarity and frank intention to compromise. The publication itself and the manner in which it was presented were distasteful. I felt that following such a path was impossible and indecent for me. For this reason I rang Yeltsin and said: 'We have a film of your appearance in the States at the university and we're intending to air it on Central Television. I understand that its reception will have implications and that's why I'm letting you know because I didn't want to do this behind your back.' I also said that if he wanted we were prepared to show it in advance to him personally or to one of his people. The answer was 'No thanks, I'll take a look at it myself.' Following the preview (on that very same day) Yeltsin rang me and said that the film didn't leave any room for optimism and it would be best not to air it at all. I explained that I couldn't keep if off the air as I wouldn't be able to explain why television was mute on this scandalous matter. In response Yeltsin asked me whether, if I had to air the tape, could I please air not just the appearance where he didn't appear in the best light, but also other meetings in the US. We fulfilled Yeltsin's request and selected some more material from what we had and aired it all in one broadcast so as to remove any hint at partiality.

As is well known, allegations that the film had been fabricated at Ostankino by altering the playing speed appeared in print later. There was nothing at all behind these allegations. It was just a run-of-the-mill ploy in the political struggle and everyone who had anything to do with television understood that quite well as the televised recording was of a meeting, not simply a monologue presentation. A meeting, as is well known, involves many people moving, asking questions and talking at the same time. Technically it just isn't possible to alter at will the behaviour and speech of one individual without affecting the others.

The second episode in which Central Television and I, as chairman of Gosteleradio, turned out to be the reason behind a conflict with Boris Yeltsin took place in June 1990 when the First Congress of People's Deputies of the RSFSR was in session. If I am not mistaken, it was the seventh of June when I was called by Yeltsin's secretariat and asked to record his appearance on the eighth of June in order to present him on television either that day or on the ninth of June. I replied that we were prepared to do so but as far as the time of the broadcast was concerned it was clear we wouldn't be able to air it that day. So I said that we would air it at a convenient hour on the ninth or tenth of June either before the *Vremya* (Time) news show or directly after, a time slot normally considered favourable for the appearances of state leaders. After the recording was made, it became known to me that Gorbachev was already scheduled to appear on the ninth. In order to separate these two appearances and not air both on the same day, I made the decision to air Yeltsin's appearance on the tenth of June, taking into consideration the fact that his speech didn't contain anything of great urgency and also that from the very beginning this possibility had not been ruled out. I am writing about this in spring 1992 at a time when passions are at fever pitch at the Fifth Congress of People's Deputies of Russia and at each session members of parliament are furiously demanding a crack-down on the mass media. What was taking place in my time were the first signs, the first cracks to mar Russian democracy. The morning of the ninth of June, after it had become known from the newspapers that the television broadcast of Boris Yeltsin's appearance had not been planned, the subject of discrimination against the Chairman of the Supreme Soviet of the RSFSR on the part of USSR Gosteleradio was raised at the session of the congress. In the morning Ruslan Khasbulatov, the first deputy Chairman of the Supreme Soviet of the RSFSR, rang me and asked to advise the congress on this matter. I replied that there had been no discrimination and that I was prepared to explain this to the congress.

In connection with the passions which were building up at the congress, I was asked at that time to go see Gorbachev and inform him of the heart of the matter. Around eleven o'clock I was in Gorbachev's office on Staraya Square and told him about the essence of the conflict, which he had not been aware of until then. He heard me out and agreed with what I was saying. After our meeting, I didn't waste any time but went straight to the Grand Kremlin Palace and asked to be given the floor. I was offered the opportunity to say a few words in an atmosphere of deliberately heated up irritation on the part of certain deputies who were obviously looking for a subject to create a scandal with the aim of deepening the rift between Gorbachev and Yeltsin. Standing face to face with the hostile audience of the congress, I was forced to muster all my will power and composure in order to keep the peace and deal with everything that had fallen on my head.

Gazing around the hall at those who wanted so much to humiliate me, I thought about how correct I was never to play any kind of games with powerful leaders, to have my own opinion and always to make independent decisions and to take responsibility for them as well. The sharp dialogue with Russian deputies on this occasion reinforced my conviction that they held a low opinion of us government officials and ministers who allegedly changed with the weather, capable only of fawning upon Gorbachev and not able to act or make decisions independently. I saw that my argument that the decision to air Yeltsin's appearance on the tenth of June was made by me alone without consulting anyone else met a poor reception. To the extent of their own prejudices they didn't believe me even though I was telling the truth. They didn't believe me even when I explained that if I were to take part in the conflict between the two leaders, I would be taking on a dangerous mission and would find myself in a difficult position. More readily they accepted the argument that there hadn't been anything extraordinary about Yeltsin's speech and postponing it for one day could in no way undermine its relevance or effect. A fact they could convince themselves of on the following day. And that's what happened.

After watching Yeltsin's speech on television the following day, the deputies didn't ask me another question and didn't consider it necessary to bring up the subject again. Boris Yeltsin, who was presiding over the congress, heard my calm arguments and I believe he was among those who believed that I had in fact made the decision concerning the time of the broadcast independently. In any case he understood that the conflict had already served its purpose and he would no longer stir up any passion.

The opposition of different political forces in the struggle for power at times took the form of clashes for possession of the airwaves on television. An example of this was the event of April 6, 1990 when a group of deputies from the Leningrad Soviet numbering about twenty or thirty people, who acted in sheer disregard of the opinion of USSR Gosteleradio and the Supreme Soviet of the USSR, occupied the studio and started broadcasting live on the Leningrad channel, having locked up B. Petrov, the chairman of the regional committee of radio and television, in his own office. This seizure was preceded by a two-day debate in the Supreme Soviet of the USSR in the Committee on Ethics on the subject of the speech of the well-known radical, deputy to the Supreme Soviet of the USSR, Nikolai Ivanov (a member of Gdlyan's group of investigators) exposing the Central Committee of the Communist Party of the Soviet Union and the President of the USSR as accomplices in the well-known Uzbek case on corruption. In consideration of the fact that the committee of the USSR Supreme Soviet headed by Roy Medvedev was working on the matter concerning the Gdlyan-Ivanov group, the decision was made to institute a temporary moratorium on coverage of the theme in the mass media. The USSR Gosteleradio carried out this decision and gave the Leningrad committee the order to refrain from televising the appearances of Nikolai Ivanov.

The seizure of the studio and the unauthorised broadcast on the Leningrad channel which functioned as the fifth all-Union channel (as its transmissions covered, apart from the North-West, the Baltic republics and Central Russia, the Volga regions up to the Urals) once again put me in a position, as chairman of Gosteleradio, of having to make a decision of major importance independently. I did not agree with those people who thought that one could simply make use of prohibitive technical means and shut down the broadcast of the Leningrad channel to the Soviet Union, having limited this unauthorised appearance to only the local city audience. I did not agree as it was alien to me to give the mere semblance of bold action and therefore I made the decision not to shut down the broadcast so that this appearance could be a fact revealing the true situation at Central Television.

A few days later I had to report on this event at a meeting of the Politburo of the CC CPSU. I stated that television could not take upon itself the functions of state power and decide for the Leningrad Soviet and party organs who should appear on radio and television and when. Certain members of the Politburo obviously did not like my comment that the debate on the investigative activities of Gdlyan and Ivanov had been going on a year already and that many committees had been created yet there had been no decision or conclusion reached convincing to public opinion. As a result the case had long ago become an object in the political struggle, a factor which was being used to destabilise the situation in the country, and Central Television had become a direct instrument in these political games.

In actual fact, for over two years by that time, Gdlyan and Ivanov, using the classical method of the political bluff, had been threatening to bring to the public eye the facts known to them alone of corruption of the higher party echelon with Gorbachev, Ligachev and Grishin implicated in it, but each time they got an opportunity to tell all they knew their speech invariably ended with general arguments and hypotheses. It is now clear to everyone that they were simply deceiving the trusting Soviet people with the sole aim of destabilising the Centre and gaining personal notoriety and political weight, and they were successful in achieving this. I believe that the names of Gdlyan and Ivanov will long remain as most crafty in that time of troubles.

In consideration of the critical situation in the country and the fact that Gosteleradio had no rights at all, I insisted at that session of the CC CPSU Politburo on the creation of a new structure for managing Central Television and Radio. The old centralised administrative system of management was obsolete and had become an anachronism. In the editorial departments of radio and television the same bitter struggle was going on as was taking place in the Supreme Soviet of the USSR, in the republics, in Moscow and Leningrad. Under these circumstances it was not possible to carry out the work of Gosteleradio by following administrative instructions and the directions given by Gorbachev and his staff over the telephone as to what to air on Central Television and what to keep off the air.

The Politburo members did not respond with any optimism to my suggestions, but the decision was made to assign Vadim Medvedev, Nikolai Ryzhkov and Yevgeni Primakov the task of carefully studying the situation at radio and television and submitting to Gosteleradio their proposals on improving the administrative structure. In order to learn the state of affairs, a week later the USSR Council of Ministers listened to my presentation of the situation at Central Television and once again, for the umpteenth time, had I the chance to see for myself that Nikolai Ryzhkov's deputies had a poor grasp of the complicated processes which had been going on in the country. The basic motive of their speeches (Doguzhiev's, Mostovoi's, Lavyorov's) and the arguments in defence of the administrative prohibition on appearances of all those people not agreeable to the government boiled down to the idea that television was state-run and financed out of the state budget, therefore it was its duty to defend all the actions of the Council of Ministers. I recall that it was probably for the first time that I did not hold back in my presentation when responding to questions at the Council of Ministers, and spoke sharply about the political shortsightedness of the government leaders and of the failure to understand that, in the face of general collapse and the bitter struggle in the country, television could not be biased or serene, as it was a mirror in which society sees a reflection of its own blemishes and abhors them. The leaders of the USSR Council of Ministers did not understand that the harsh critical appearances on the Moscow and Leningrad channels, on the second Russian television programme, which were predominated by the political forces in opposition to the Union government, were a reality not of television but of life itself.

Soon after the Politburo session I had a frank conversation with Ryzhkov, who was one of the few in the Council of Ministers who understood the sources of the events taking place and was aware of their unmanageability and inevitability. I saw how much he was tortured by a dissatisfaction with the weakening of executive power, how he suffered from the fact that the government without the support of the President of the USSR was losing ever more control over the economic and political processes in the country. In answer to my question of what to do in this dead-end situation he replied: 'Preserve one's honour and conscience and follow one's road to the end – not for the sake of power, which is too heavy a burden now, but for the sake of Motherland, something which we all have in common.'

It became increasingly difficult for me to maintain mutual relations on the old administrative basis with the creative editorial departments and the various television shows and broadcasts. The opposition to the official authorities, to the Supreme Soviet of the USSR, the President of the USSR, and the USSR Council of Ministers received ever-greater support from below, especially in Moscow and Leningrad. The shrinking authority of the CPSU accelerated the process. This is the only way to explain why twelve leading TV journalists, predominantly from the programmes that spoke out in opposition to the official authorities, were elected deputies to the Supreme Soviet of the RSFSR, three of whom were presenters of the show *Vzglyad* (Viewpoint). More and more often at the press conferences I held regularly journalists would ask me whether I regretted that I had taken on my shoulders such a heavy burden as Gosteleradio. In reply I tried to keep my spirits up and would answer that regret was unproductive, that it was necessary to work. But work was getting more and more difficult as it had already become impossible to resist through regular means the extremism which was sweeping the Central Television broadcasts.

Soviet television, in breaking loose from the administrative fetters of party and state control, had at the same time fallen into another extreme: it had become the platform for expressing subjective group views and evaluations and with its prejudices had increasingly exerted pressure on public opinion. Gosteleradio was receiving more and more letters in which television viewers expressed their concern that many broadcasts and presenters obviously lacked objectivity in their evaluation of events. In their letters to Gosteleradio people expressed their concern over the fact that, in the conditions of destabilisation of society and deepening of economic, social and ethnic crises, mass media, particularly the most powerful and influential ones – radio and television, were primarily acting as agents of destruction rather than creation. In my regular meetings with radio and television editors I spoke many times about how great a privilege it was to engage in dialogue with millions of people and how it was necessary for them to consider the question of what aims and what intentions are pursued by particular programmes and broadcasts.

In my efforts to be objective I understood very well that, when a violent struggle among various public views and forces was going on and when every social ill long concealed by a veneer of well-being was being exposed to the greatest degree, television could not be better than its time and it could not embellish the reality of the situation. As a professional political analyst, having worked for many years in the mass media, I could not fail to know that any position, no matter how truthful or honest, when it was a matter of millions of people would elicit the support of some and the enmity of others. On the other hand, I was experienced and I saw that the destruction, exposure and criticism of all and sundry could not and must not remain for such a long time the sole priority of mass media and prevail so long over creative processes. I was aware that people's ordinary day-to-day life with its joys and sorrows, hopes and disappointments carried on away from the television screen. The everyday life of the working city, village and family and the lot of man in the street disappeared from the television screen.

The reader cannot help but notice that this is not the first time my thoughts have turned to the theme of creation and destruction in the mass media. Today it has become even more topical than at that time of which I am writing since the monopoly and triumph of group prejudices in television broadcasts have reached the extreme limit.

In my view such a powerful means of influence on mass consciousness as television (however it may try to be neutral and objective) has to strive to prepare public opinion for the idea of the democratic renewal of the life in the country. And its most important task in this connection is to return to the people the lost sense of being masters of their own fate and homeland, to free them from their slavish submission and obedience and to help them overcome the egalitarianism which is destructive to human dignity. I am talking with conviction: nothing in our current degrading, paltry existence will change if changes do not take place in the most important sphere of human activity, namely labour. The most civilised and democratic, the most humane and perfect social relations by themselves do not guarantee people happiness and a decent life, they only guarantee the possibility of achieving them. To instil belief in the creative omnipotence of man, the creator of his own happiness, no matter how tragic or depressing our current situation, is one of the primary social functions of television. And now, when there is an outbreak of meetings and pickets, at Ostankino as well, my opinions only confirm the truth that television should serve ordinary people and depend only on them.

Nobody doubts that the basic task of television is news. The effectiveness of news is always determined by accuracy and the speed of its dissemination. The superiority of television here is beyond doubt. Perestroika, with its democratic processes and the sharpness of their delineation, made information the most important element of social life and conditioned its plurality and its contradictory nature. The influence of news programmes and the huge interest in them across the country have grown enormously.

But the twists and turns of television news remain inscrutable in our country. Given the national fondness for the rule of extremes and their place in the forefront of argument, coupled with disdain for common sense, news programmes will always remain one of the weapons in the sharp political struggle between various social forces. I think that this is also a result of the fact that for too long news in our country was controlled and meted out by the Communist Party. As a result, television proved absolutely unprepared to reflect the plurality of information which resulted from perestroika.

Anyone who watches the news carefully would agree with me that the pressing problems facing the people who put it together have still not been solved. There is no attempt to ensure objectivity and a healthy balance between information and commentary. As in the past, priority is given to a subjective interpretation of events with the obligatory and obtrusive judgements and evaluations of presenters. Broadening the information space on television has not changed this. Creating new news programmes – Television News Service (TNS) and the Russian informational programme *Vesti* (The News) – has only increased the scope for subjective interference by journalists in the content of information and its interpretation.

Changes in the leadership of Central Television and the news departments have changed nothing. News, judging by many new programmes, is a competitive experiment in the limits of what is permitted and what can be said, a search for the edge of ethical acceptability in the evaluations of events and actions, of the personal qualities of the leaders of movements and parties, and of social activists. Commenting on this trend, the television director Vladimir Maximov, writing in *Pravda*, noted harshly but justifiably: 'Today many mix up professionalism with reportorial rudeness.' The acknowledged leaders in this type of information programmes competition have become famous. The new generation of commentators, news analysts and presenters were born of these unsettled time of change. They include Tatyana Mitkova, Svetlana Sorokina, Yuri Rostov, Yevgeny Kiselev, and Vladislav Flyarkovsky. They have become both popular and notorious for their subjective frankness which often is no more than the most basic violation of the generally accepted norms and principles of the informational genre: objectivity, neutrality, non-interference in the content and evaluation of ongoing facts and events. Viewers today keep insisting on more facts and less words in the television news so that they can make their own choices between news and commentary. Viewers demand with ever more persistence that presenters stop supplying them with ready answers.

The new forms of information programmes characteristic of our times find their clearest expression in the work of Alexander Nevzorov and his television programme *600 Seconds*. On the one hand, I feel that his work clearly reflects an undoubted courage, outstanding talent and the highest professional qualities of a presenter. On the other hand, there is an open subjectivism, the triumph of personal bias, and a desire to foist his own point of view on public opinion. Over the years I have been watching *600 Seconds*, I have come to value its position. I can see the mastery of a professional reporter, unobtainable for others, and I understand how difficult it is for Nevzorov to do what he is doing, how difficult it is to go against the grain, to defend, in conditions of sharp confrontation, the national dignity of ethnic Russians in the Baltic countries and Moldavia... At the same time, I cannot but acknowledge that then and now I do not completely agree with his professional approach. I do not agree with the shock tone of his reportage, the categorical nature of his statements and criticisms. The so-called 'shock information' of which Nevzorov is a proponent is of course sharp and emotional. It moves people and does not leave them indifferent. However today, when people even without this are in dire straits, tired of disorder and ruin, tragedy and loss, do we really need to turn especially to 'shock information' in our television reportage?

The Spiritual Mission of Television

Influencing popular convictions is in practice the most complex function of radio and television. Its success depends on the level of professionalism and civic responsibility of journalists, their moral and ethical standards, competency and intelligence. Here the question arises of social guidelines for the mass media and the aims they pursue in their publications and broadcasts. To the question: should television persuade?, I answer with a second question: in these difficult times, should it help people establish a balanced point of view and confidence in tomorrow, or as in the past should it only set out to destroy and deepen social conflicts, pushing social forces into confrontation involving force, even civil war?

I remember how much doubt and open derision met my claim that television is called on to comfort the people. But anybody who was not blind and deaf, who saw and felt the pain and suffering of his or her fellow countrymen, could not but acknowledge how insistent was the need of our sick society for a spiritual comforter. Who could claim to this role? Who could render a healthy influence on the moral atmosphere, and help discharge the irritation accumulated in our society? Of course, television doesn't have a monopoly on answers to these questions, but in fulfilling its spiritual mission it can do more than any one person. Look at how much anxiety and doubt has built up in society, how painfully people perceive the dramatic events in society. This is why the necessity for effective interference in the moral atmosphere of society is so urgent. To ignore this when speaking about the social mission of the omnipotent television, in my opinion, would be in our times a serious mistake.

Everyone remembers how much criticism was levelled at Gosteleradio for giving Anatoli Kashpirovsky and Allan Chumak access to the airwaves. On the other hand, it was obvious that the enormous and devoted interest in these controversial shows was without doubt connected with the spiritual confusion which had gripped society at the time. Shifts in spiritual orientation, the re-evaluation of cultural values, the difficult adjustment to new moral criteria – all this required television to take an active concern in the spiritual defence of man.

No man is ever a prophet in his own country. In defence of the spiritual mission of television, I fall back on the authority of the most famous prophet of Russia, Alexander Solzhenitsyn. In his notes written while still abroad, *How We Must Rebuild Russia*, he notes: 'Political life is far from the most important form of a person's life, politics is hardly the choice of occupation for the majority. The more sweeping is political life in the country, the more spiritual life is lost. Politics should not swallow up the spiritual forces of the nation and its leisure time which otherwise could have been devoted to creative activities.' I am convinced and for this reason continue to insist that the spiritual mission of television is never so relevant as in times of popular misfortune and suffering. There are eternal concepts – good and evil, honour and conscience, love and hate, human dignity and charity – which television must constantly bring to the viewer to remind him or her what it means to be a human being. Remind him or her so that man does not descend into baseness and evil and lose faith in the triumph of justice and good.

Not only did I ponder the spiritual mission of television, but I tried to put several of my ideas into practice. As a result the weekly programme *Sunday's Ethical Sermons* was started. The first shows showed that there was an enormous amount of interest in them. But they were difficult to make: it was not an easy task to find authors capable of affecting the delicate strings of the human soul.

It became evident that there was an obvious shortage of professionalism, talent, spiritual forces and heartfelt sympathy for the man who had fallen on hard times in his own country. The sermons worked which were conducted by people who were closer to the themes professionally – teachers, priests, writers. It was in one of these Sunday sermons that Father Alexander Men, who later was tragically killed, became famous.

Professional limitations were evident not only in *Sunday Sermons*. Both the long running morning show *120 Minutes* and the desperately-needed *30 Minutes Before Sleep* (which could have been called *Goodnight Adults* after the wonderful children's show *Goodnight Kiddies*) could effectively have served as a moral comfort for the people, and helped them weather the storms of social passions had there been the desire and professionalism.

In order to prepare the necessary proposals for changes in the structure of Gosteleradio and its relationship with the authorities and political organisations (first of all the CPSU), a fundamental state decision was needed. Consultations with and the advice of Nikolai Ryzhkov helped. I should point out that even when relations with the government were at their most complicated, and the government was being mercilessly accused of everything and anything on Central Radio and Television by both the USSR and Russian Federation People's Deputies, and the leaders of the Democratic Russia movement, Ryzhkov was one of few who invariably held to a position of common sense and kept up the very best of relations with me. With his help, we prepared a special decree of the President of the USSR on the necessity for serious structural changes at television, which, after discussing them with me, Gorbachev also agreed to.

On the 14th of July, 1990, the Presidential Decree entitled *On the Democratisation and Development of Television and Radio in the USSR* was issued. It reflected those positions which I have spoken about above. They included the task of developing the USSR Law on Radio and Television, of preserving and developing them as nationwide structures capable within the framework of the democratisation of society of reflecting the really existing political pluralism. The main proposition of the decree, that the functions of state-run television and radio had to be carried out independently of political and public organisations and serve the objective coverage of the processes taking place in the country, with a special emphasis that the monopolisation of air time by one or another party, political movement or group, was unacceptable, was met with interest though not without misgivings, especially among the functionaries of the CPSU Central Committee. In order to preserve their monopoly rights, some of television's professionals, while supporting this provision, voiced concern about the thesis noting the unacceptability of turning state television into a vehicle for the propagation of the personal political views of the workers of Gosteleradio. In the proposals concerning the democratisation of Central Television the most important thing for us was the task set in the Presidential Decree for the State Committee for Television and Radio to reorganise its activity with the aim of promoting the fuller and freer expression of the creative potential of TV and radio workers and promoting the development of democratic principles. In order to achieve this, the USSR Gosteleradio was granted the permission to enter into labour agreements with its workers on a contractual and competitive basis.

How did I myself see the changes in the structure of Central Radio and Television? I shall go into some detail here since I feel that the point is still relevant today. Through a process of exchange of opinions with the work collectives of the main departments and in meetings with the editors-in-chief we prepared proposals according to which each television channel would become creatively and commercially independent and receive a particular thematic and professional orientation. Channel One would become the official, predominantly socio-political and information channel to perform general state tasks where information programmes would naturally combine with high-quality entertainment. Channel Two was intended to cater for the needs of Russian Television which was still in its formative stages. We therefore considered it expedient to retain on this channel programmes of the Union republics and of Russian local television studios. Channel Three, the Moscow channel, would be awarded to the capital and become a municipal channel, but its creative and technical links with Central Television would be retained. The proposals for the reorganisation of Channel Four, the so-called general educational channel, aroused a lot of interest. Generalising from the practice and experience of educational television, Eduard Sagalaev put forward a number of proposals which we subsequently approved outlining the creation on Channel Four of the first 'social television' company. It was to be called *21st Century TV*.

In theory this was a serious step towards democratisation and the creation of a really alternative television. It was envisaged that on a joint-stock basis the founders of this 'social television' would become the Culture Foundation, the USSR Academy of Sciences, the Ministry for Culture and the State Committee for Education as well as other public, union and youth organisations. Content-wise we talked about making programmes that would set high cultural, ethical and intellectual standards. Airtime was intended to be mainly devoted to the introduction of a wide audience to the achievements of world civilisation, culture, art and science. The object was to unite the creative efforts of directors, scriptwriters, authors and editors attracted by the ideas of enlightenment and spiritual selfless labour. For all the suspicion which some television professionals greeted this idea with, I felt it was one of the most interesting and fruitful since I admit for me the ideal of television was not political but enlightening and spiritual, a place where literature, art and music should rule. I am glad that this idea of Sagalaev's began to come to life on Channel Six in the form of an independent television company with the participation of the well-known TV magnate, CNN's Ted Turner, though it started only two and a half years later, on January 1, 1993. Interviewed by *Moscow News*, Sagalaev said that his aim was to create a new form of family-oriented informational and entertainment television, depending only on the viewer. My motto, he said, is popularity and culture.

In our proposals we also included Channel Five, the Leningrad channel. Its viewing audience was nationwide and we felt it should be independent as far as its creative efforts and production issues were concerned while continuing to work closely with Central Television. Under the proposed structure, all programming was to be planned and managed on the basis of fully independent channels.

To this end and according to our plan a board of directors was set up at each of the channels which determined the content of programmes in accordance with the channel's specialisation. It was vitally important that the new structure acknowledge the creative and legal independence of the main departments which were to develop their relations with the different channels on a contractual and competitive basis. This would amount to a death knell for the monopoly of the main departments and signal the end for mediocre programmes whose existence for many years now had simply been maintained by administrative fiat. The new structure favoured those departments which did not fear competition, had initiative and could air their product not on one channel alone but on any channel and in this way supplant grey and mediocre programmes.

The appearance of five channels, all creatively autonomous, would in my opinion bring about serious changes in the administrative system of Gosteleradio and would create favourable conditions for the airing of programmes with various viewpoints and opinions. These changes really did open up the possibility for the appearance of alternative programmes.

Our proposals, of course, were constrained in their radicalism. They bore the stamp of the times and did not touch upon the main issue – to whom did Central Television belong? This question was fundamental since everything else depended on how it was answered. At the time, public opinion had already tried to answer the question of who owned television. Eduard Sagalaev maintained that state television belonged neither to the government nor to the president (*Pravda*, April 6, 1990). This was a fair opinion but it could not lead to any solution since the owners and structure of Soviet television from the very beginning were different from those in any other country where a leading role was played by state television (Britain, Japan, Finland...). Soviet television differed in that in reality it was not the state that owned it but rather the administrative governmental system or, more to the point, the party and government. Today, when it has ceased to belong to the Communist Party, it is fully controlled by the presidential and government structures.

I point this out since arguments about the independence of

television and whether it belongs to the state have been heatedly debated from the time of the First Congress of People's Deputies of the USSR in 1990. The polemics reached a high point at the Sixth Congress of People's Deputies of Russia in April 1992. Carefully analysing the contents of this polemic, I saw that unfortunately it was not a debate about professional issues since nothing at all was being said about the real 'owner' of state television, the viewer. Television had been carved up and continues to be carved up by the executive and legislative branches of power. Meanwhile, international practice shows that television is truly independent only when it does not depend on parties, the government or parliament but depends on the people, and when there are definite parliamentary mechanisms which serve this end and ensure that this dependence really exists.

As chairman of the USSR Gosteleradio I studied the administrative mechanisms of the state televisions of Japan, Finland and Italy, visiting these countries and inviting to Moscow the heads of their state-run television companies. Discussions with these people and meeting Western editors, directors and programme makers convinced me that television there had indeed a certain degree of independence in its relationship with the executive and legislative powers. The basis of this independence is the financial independence of television since the portion of the state budget allocated to television does not play a significant role. The main source of finance for state television is the viewer who renews his television licence annually. And it is this that guarantees the immediate dependence of television on the viewer and its independence with respect to the government.

I also point out that I have never heard from any of my Western colleagues, heads of television companies, the claim to being the fourth power, but at the same time it was obvious that they are not entirely dependent on the government and ruling parties since the work of state television is coordinated and controlled in these countries by parliament which has a special supervisory council or committee drawn from the various parties. This parliamentary organ controls the time made available on television to the various parties and social movements as well as the time allowed for advertising (state television in many of these countries has very little if no advertising at all). It also ensures a healthy proportion of foreign and local programming.

Anyone who knows anything about our television would agree with me that no even remotely similar organ has been created here. And all the lengthy debates in the press and in parliament about people's television and its independence in my opinion don't make any sense, they are only camouflage – a cover-up of the total dependency of television on the government and its inevitable partiality. Any denial of the absolute pro-government orientation of our television can arouse nothing but irony since it is simply absurd to talk of television which is obliged by the Constitution to defend the policies of the state, as somehow being in opposition to either the President, government or parliament.

I shall allow myself a digression here in the hope that it will not be without interest for the reader. Today's Central Television in its existing form only mimics a plurality of opinions, remaining, as the case was formerly, a one-party television. I believe it is only cunning or lack of knowledge of world practice that could explain the statement by the head of Central Television Ostankino, Yegor Yakovlev, at a press conference following the end of the Sixth Congress of People's Deputies of Russia, which was devoted to the independence of state-run television. He said then that parliaments and people's deputies come and go, but the mass media and television in effect never go. In actual fact, this was only a *mot*, a fairly worn-out one, and incorrect into the bargain: it is true that the mass media, including television, do not go, but their leaders do. Ironically fate decreed that Yakovlev should not even remain head of Ostankino up to the opening of the Seventh Congress of People's Deputies of Russia.

If our conscience has not abandoned us finally, then we cannot but acknowledge how much ill our all-powerful television has brought people in recent years: replacing the theatre, the concert hall, the library, museums and the cinema. How much rubbish, pornography and baseness, especially in the last year, it has churned out for the viewer. How active and purposeful has been the process of destruction of all our former values and authorities, the mockery of our spiritual heritage, of the dignity of the nation, the country, the people. I believe that damage done by the destructive activities of our television which it is engaged in day by day, hour by hour, by its evil will, is for the most part irreparable. Let us be honest: women endlessly parading themselves half-naked in the name of beauty contests, endless calls, from people of all ages, to make money and the extolling of anything 'Western', all this is not so harmless and leaves a definite imprint on our life. The day will eventually come when our country and its people will have lost their dignity and been deprived of their identity. I am writing this with a bitter sense of my own involvement and guilt which I must live with till the end of my life.

When fate was not being kind to him, my grandfather would often say that man supposes and God proposes. The thoughts and decisions of our leaders, like the ways of God, are inscrutable. The Presidential Decree on the democratisation of television which we thought would launch important structural changes, in effect turned out to be a fig leaf, covering Gorbachev's real intentions. Parallel to what we in Gosteleradio were thinking, arguing furiously at the sessions of our Board and in the main departments about what Central Television ought to be and nurturing the idea of its democratisation, Gorbachev and his inner circle, without consulting us or even bothering to put us in the picture, were seeking their own solution in secret. As usual, they assumed that they knew everything, understood everything and knew exactly that what they had to do was the traditional thing – replace the head. I watch Gorbachev on television today (for instance, his recent appearance in the *Red Square* programme with Alexander Lyubimov in October 1992), and hearing his long-winded reflections on different ways of thinking and of his devotion to glasnost I cannot but note once again that politics is not made in snow-white gloves and that it is out of step with moral norms. Gorbachev's patience with me was exhausted. He began searching for a new head for the USSR Gosteleradio, someone capable of more obedience, someone who wouldn't ask too many questions.

In Russia it has long been the case that rumours come before state decisions. Already in September 1990, my 'well-wishers' at television began to whisper to me in great secret that Gorbachev's closest advisors were actively insisting on changes in the leadership of Gosteleradio. Apparently they had already secured the support of Alexander Yakovlev though it was Yevgeny Primakov, the President's chief of mass media, who was in charge of the whole operation. The only thing, according to my 'well-wishers', that was holding up things was the absence of consensus about who should be the new chairman. I have never been a specialist of these cloak and dagger games. I wasn't one for intrigues and never ingratiated myself with the President's advisors, though I was well aware that it was in fact they who cooked this kind of things connected with new appointments. I also knew that my enemies amongst the General Secretary's advisors had already put together a number of reports about Nenashev's liberalism, his unwillingness to use an iron hand to bring the situation at television under control. Some of these reports which Gorbachev then passed on to the Central Committee telling them to deal with them came my way and I still have them, living evidence of the intrigues.

In October 1990, Gorbachev stopped receiving me. He sent his orders and complaints (which he still had) by way of his advisors. Knowing his intentions, I did not insist on a meeting, I knew that we would not be able to reach an understanding since we had clearly parted ways. I also did not try to meet the people who might have been able to influence his decision: Yakovlev, Primakov, Dzasokhov. I had nothing to ask for, I felt that to try and explain what was happening at Central Television would have been pointless since I had already said everything that needed saying and moreover they might interpret it as a person desperate to hold onto office.

Now, two years later, it is even clearer to me that Gorbachev's attempts to muzzle television were void of any sense and born of an ignorance of the real state of affairs in the country's information centre. To this day I cannot fully understand the mechanism of formulation of decisions such as this, at the heart of which lies distrust for people and contempt for their opinions and knowledge. I am talking about this here not at all because I was offended, since at the time I had made no secret of my desire to leave Gosteleradio. What I didn't understand was why the opinion of a person who only a year and a half earlier had been entrusted with so serious and responsible a piece of work, was no longer considered worth listening to on so complex an issue as the situation in the information sphere.

On November 11, Alexander Dzasokhov – a secretary of the CPSU Central Committee whom Gorbachev had asked to keep an eye on television – telephoned me and said that the Soviet President wanted to see both of us. We met in Dzasokhov's office in the Central Committee and since we both were well aware of what the meeting was going to be about exchanged opinions. I said that personally I was relieved to be leaving television, but that I could not pretend that a change of leadership would do anything except make the situation worse at Gosteleradio since it was the administrative structure that needed to be changed and not the chief administrator. Dzasokhov agreed with my point of view and asked me to try and convince Gorbachev that this was the case.

My conversation with the Soviet President was formal and diplomatic. Gorbachev spoke of how well he thought of me and how important it was for me now to take up my old work but with a new orientation and to concentrate on preparing a proposal for the creation of a Soviet Ministry of Information and the Press. He listened to my evaluation and notes about the situation at television without interest. It was clear that the new structure and our proposals were of little interest to him, since, as he pointed out, he was counting on the decisiveness of Leonid Kravchenko and his previous experience.

Again I had the feeling at this last meeting that Gorbachev, to his misfortune and that of the country, lacked what was most basic in good leadership – the ability to listen to people. He only really listened carefully to himself. As a result he was not in a position to understand that television was an adequate reflection of the situation in the country as a whole. In his understanding of the situation in the sphere of mass media, Gorbachev could not overcome the long formed impressions of the provincial secretary of the Stavropol Territorial Committee of the CPSU, and there was no one who could help him here. Something I could never understand at the time was why he still wanted to keep me in the government. I'm talking about this since at this last meeting with him I asked to be released back to scientific work at the Academy of Social Sciences where for a long time I had worked as a professor and was a member of the academic council. He answered that he could not agree to this request since very difficult times were at hand and he needed those who set out with him in 1985 on the road of change, follow this road to the end. Whether these words were the result of intuition about his coming defeat or fear of being left utterly alone, I don't know, but I vouch for their validity.

Why did I agree to stay in the government and return to my earlier post in the Committee for the Press? I returned because I still hoped to finish my plans for changes in the field of publishing. I had kept up my contacts with publishers and knew that a lot had remained there much as when I had left it. And I returned because I still did not fully realise that the government was in its death throes. The blind man loses his crutch only once and when Gorbachev lost his last executive crutch – the USSR Council of Ministers, it signalled the end of the Centre's executive power and put the Soviet President in a position of a helpless blind man.

Gorbachev's appointment of Leonid Kravchenko to the post of head of Gosteleradio authorised to fulfil the Soviet President's will seemed a hopeless move at the time. His short sojourn in the role of chairman only accelerated the processes of deformation and confrontation at Central Television. His attempts to retain the administrative reins over television were doomed. Watching this senseless struggle which only helped those who were interested in the final destabilisation of society and discreditation of the Centre's power, I had nothing but pity for the man awarded this 'highest' of honours – that of being a victim.

By the ancient nasty tradition which still holds sway today, none of those who came to the Calvary of television after me, showed the slightest interest in what their predecessor had been doing and what had prevented him from carrying his cross. Nothing has changed – nobody wants to learn from the past or even understand it.

The time which fate allotted me in television was, fortunately, short, and I don't consider it wasted since it taught me a lot. It enriched my understanding of myself, of people who shared my burden, and of the leaders of this country in those fateful times.

Chapter 6 – Illusions of Freedom

The Heavy Burden of a Loyal Performer

It is fair to say that after a victory the battle field is usually left in the hands of looters. It turned out that our fanciful notions during perestroika about how our lives would take shape after we had rid ourselves of the administrative totalitarian regime and rejected Party hegemony had very little in common with what actually happened in reality. Freedom from the dictates of the administrative command centre and from the CPSU was purely an idealised dream.

We were filled with the naive expectation that freedom would sort everything out itself, and the child of freedom – the coveted market – would form, organise and arrange everything. But the officially declared freedom has reigned triumphant for two years now and we have seen our idealised dream first dim and then turn into something utterly absurd. The state institutes armed with a multitude of draft laws have been unable to protect man and he cannot take advantage of the proclaimed freedom. And freedom itself has turned before our very eyes into the uncontrolled freedom of violence, robbery, endless stealing and legalised bribery.

What has happened to us and our country? How can it be that contemporary democratic power which proclaimed equality, justice and the uncompromised struggle against privileges has not only failed to abolish privileges, but multiplied them manifold. In comparison with Russia's dying public health system, to which, according to official data, a mere 1.8 billion roubles is currently allocated, government apparatus maintenance already costs several billion rubles. Why, having destroyed the centre, have we an even more unwieldy, expensive and primarily self-serving bureaucratic machine built on the remains of the old state structures?

How can it be that, as a result of the reforms carried out for the common good, more than 70% of the country's population, also according to the 1992 data of statisticians and sociologists, are living on the poverty line and the nation is beginning to die out? For the first time in many years, as a result of the country's social catastrophe, more people are dying than being born. According to the statistics for 1992, the population of Russia has decreased by more than 70,000 people, and the number of births has decreased by almost 200,000, and there were 185,000 more deaths than births.

Or were our hopes of freedom only an illusion which had no chance of becoming a reality? Or is freedom really only a perceived necessity strictly protected by the state? I would like to note in this connection that in our intention to live according to the norms of universal human morals, we should understand that all the distortions of our reality which are currently making our lives unbearable, the turbid wave of crime, thievery, bribery and corruption at all levels of power, are not rooted in either the communist or the democratic system, they are immoral and illegal in any social relations. Everything depends on the objective conditions which promote or hinder the manifestation of all these social deformations.

I shall take the liberty of digressing here to explain my approach to the problem. A person who has been employed for many years in government service, in a system of constant complex dependencies, both party and government (of course the higher one's position, the greater one's dependency) and who is left without a job, will at first be distraught and feel out of place, reminiscent somehow of a deceived and abandoned wife or a workhorse released from the reins which for so long kept it harnessed to a heavy but familiar cart. However, very soon, if he has any common sense, he comes to understand that despite all the losses, there is the indisputable advantage of being able to analyse and closely observe those phenomena and processes of which he was previously only an obedient performer.

In my opinion, to analyse what is going on today in actual life means to distinguish that which was inevitable as a result of the natural development of society, i.e. that which happened because it could not help but happen, and to assess what is due only to our lack of skill and inability to control a particular phenomenon or process.

Man and time, this is where most things begin. It has already become an absolute rule in our country to blame time and our predecessors, those who have gone before, forgetting the well-known wisdom, 'do not judge those who walk ahead, remember that there are also those coming along behind you'. There are different ways of looking at what was in the distant or not-so-distant past; however, first of all this past has to be understood. Life is primarily the understanding of what is going on around you. A great part of present human suffering in our extremely confused lives is caused by a misunderstanding of what is going on. I hate, maintained the sage, that which I do not understand.

An assessment of what our intellectuals think about this can be found on the multitudinous pages of the periodic press and in radio and television commentaries where the same question is infinitely repeated: what is happening in our society, is it the tortuous process of renewal and restoration of Russia or, on the contrary, its collapse, destruction and ruin which signify the complete disappearance of Russian civilisation? It is utterly obvious that there is no thinker or prophet today capable of answering these questions in full. Neither are the multitude of tiresome sociological surveys of any help here, for they contain too much predetermined untruth from the beginning, and it is simply impossible to answer such complex questions using surveys.

It is impossible to second guess what will happen to us, but we are obliged to understand the evolution of our ideas about what was begun in 1985 as perestroika, not to become lost once and for all in the reference points designated then, in order to correlate the goals and intentions of six years ago with what has occurred today.

Everyone is very familiar with the three main stages which perestroika went through, they are accepted with certain reservations by most researchers. We also know that following the events of August 19-21, 1991, the word 'perestroika' disappeared from common usage and has only ever been heard again to emphasise its irretrievable death. In the meantime, we cannot get away from the question of what happened to perestroika. This question is raised and answered by Professor A. Butenko (*Kultura* newspaper of May 9, 1992). The gist of the author's point of view is that the shameful attitude of the current political leaders who were raised on the wave of the social movement of perestroika is associated with their ideas of socialism and communism. The contemporary leaders, the presidents of the now sovereign states: Yeltsin, Kravchuk, Nazarbayev, Karimov, Niyazov, Snegur, Shevardnadze, are representatives of the Party nomenklatura and, together with Gorbachev, were the leading propounders of renewed socialism.

On the other hand, when analysing the evolution of perestroika, particularly during its second stage following the 19th Party Conference, it cannot be ignored that a significant number of provincial Party leaders objected with increasing vigour to radical reforms in the sphere of economics and politics, limiting themselves to the improvement in the existing political system and economic relations.

At the same time, the democrats who obtained supremacy in several regions of Russia (Moscow, Leningrad, Sverdlovsk, Volgograd...) and in many of the USSR republics staunchly demanded pushing ahead with the transformations, directly maintaining that perestroika had already reached its limit with its acknowledgement of the socialist choice and that the matter should concern a radical change in the economic and political system. In his speech in April 1992 at the meeting of the Praesidium of the Russian Academy of Sciences, Academician Gennady Osipov particularly thought that the idea which appeared during this stage that 'the market decides all' was just a myth which lead to a refusal to develop a strategy for a scientifically based and gradual transfer to a market economy combining the government regulation and market aspects of its development. He maintained: 'The absolutism of the market and complete identification of the market economy with capitalism lead to a reconsideration of the main essence of perestroika as "the renewal of socialism". It came to be viewed as a "return to capitalism", to its first stage, primary accumulation, "untamed capitalism". And this was at a time when several civilised countries had entered a state of convergence, that is, the rational combination of elements of socialism and capitalism.'

When reflecting on what is happening to us today, the most noticeable thing is the incredible fatigue and exasperation of ordinary citizens. Fatigue from the unbearable everyday burdens, the unprecedented high prices and the concerns about how to survive.

Fatigue and exasperation from the utter lack of legal rights and unbridled anarchy, from the inability to protect one's home, family and children; fatigue and exasperation from the diffidence, inconsistency and instability of government decisions and acts, the continuing drop in production, unemployment and uncertainty about tomorrow. Finally, fatigue and exasperation at the loss of the Homeland and state, and at the humiliating inability to determine one's civil and state affiliation. Finding ourselves in the power of political passions, we forget that it is not poverty itself which wears one down, but the humiliation and dependence on those around one, the attendant destitution and loss of worth to which one can never reconcile. It is a well-known fact that man's first and foremost quality has always been his desire to be significant and worthy of others.

This state of mind is precisely the food and social fuel on which the political crisis is growing and strengthening in society, and it has still not reached its climax, despite the predictions of the professional forecasters who measure not in months, but in weeks. The climax of the political crisis is still to come, when the unbridled market prices draw an even more obvious line between the rich and poor, and social inequality becomes particularly threatening. Threatening not by normal European standards, but taking into account Russia's special features with its community culture of the distant past and collectivist psychology of recent socialism. It would not be wrong to suppose that precisely this will become the main social detonator for the explosion and basis of people's most serious moral shock and social discontent, which will also be the cause of the most unpredictable political upheavals.

Then there is the younger generation, about which we now keep shamefully quiet, for its future is now truly either deserted or dark. Is the market, with its merciless rules and determinants of living standards and the general commercialisation, good for the spiritual and moral state of society, along with the complete collapse of science, education, culture and art? The education cult has collapsed once and for all, talented young people are drifting into pure business and there are increasingly unsettling reports about the self-financing of university departments and self-recoupment by making students pay for lectures and seminars. There are reports about how, in the interests of profit, respectable publishing houses are striking the monographs of scientists and textbooks from their plans and replacing them with Chase, Christie or *Everything You Want to Know About Sex*.

In the multitude of articles about the essence of the totalitarianism of the past, its main feature is rightly distinguished as being the alienation of man from power. Of course, here the question arises, but what is happening now after we have so convincingly opened people's eyes to the many years of their being deprived of power? Even a brief analysis of the practice of public life over the past year shows the presence of no less of a gap than before between the ruling authorities and the millions of ordinary people. If the current political situation is evaluated objectively and impartially, it can be said without the slightest exaggeration that, just as before, in the recent past where there actually was alienation of power from the people and autonomy of the people's Soviets skilfully concealed by the demagogues, now, on the contrary, there is increasing isolation of the leading élite, that lives in the world of its own interests and desires which have nothing in common with the lives, concerns and interests of the majority of the nation.

One does not have to be a great forecaster in politics today to see that along with the merciless steps in economic reform and the continuation of the former social policy, the already fragile balance in the correlation of social forces is also collapsing. Support of government transformations by a few strata of the population is being wrested away once and for all, and the leading circles which hold power in the country are finding themselves essentially in isolation. Such pessimistic conclusions stem from the actual policy which is currently being conducted by those who came to power under the slogan of power to the people and the protection of the rights of the individual.

The inevitable and interrelated constituent elements of stability and reliability of any authority are strength and prestige. One cannot exist without the other, just as one cannot be substituted for the other. The dramatic events and conflicts of the Seventh and Eighth Congresses of the Russian People's Deputies is convincing proof of the almost equally great drop in both the strength and prestige of the powers-that-be. And the main reason is that the people's trust in those who were entrusted to rule the country has reached its limit.

Are there sufficiently serious reasons for this? There are, and extremely significant ones. Gaidar's exit, the formation of the Chernomyrdin government and his first steps occur under conditions of extremely low trust or lack of any sort of support from the people. Among the multitude of reports in the press during the first half of 1992 on the subject 'power and the people', perhaps one of the most noteworthy and blunt, written with pain in the heart, is Yuri Vlasov's article in *Pravda* (May 13, 1992) entitled *Coffin for Rent*. The author unambiguously evaluates the social processes occurring in the country as the 'devastation of the state and plunder of the people'. Yuri Vlasov, who cannot be accused of inconsistency of views, writes with sincere pain about how the reforms begun by the Russian parliament in 1992 have brought with them an orgy of rapacity, speculation, selling off and tearing apart of national property. The main real consequence of reform, believes the author, has become the destitution of the people, of essentially all categories: blue-collar and white-collar workers, the intelligentsia and pensioners. The matter has reached the point where the coffin for the deceased is now being rented out. With pain and rage, Vlasov notes that 'in the widespread demagogy of democracy they have neglected a "minor" detail: to ask the people whether or not they consent to plunder of the country and poverty; and now, destitute, they have been pushed onto the sidelines and await their fate, for they have found themselves defenceless and unequipped to deal with the so-called "new life".'

Our people, according to the graphic expression of academician Svyatoslav Fedorov, should really deserve a monument, like Pavlov's dog, because they have been capable of withstanding the social experiments performed on them. However, this long-suffering with which we have appeased ourselves for many years, concealing our inability to create a worthy life and characterising it as the main valour and most important feature of the people, is not without its limits. It is even more immoral to explain this tolerance of the people (such ideas are also encountered in the press) by the fact that they have never lived in plenty. For it is only one step from this idea to those who love, including the present pseudo-democrats, to greatly undervalue the ability of our people, their professional acumen, their talents, explaining much of the current misfortune and unhappiness in the country by lack of will, inertia, traditional Russian idleness and laziness! And this is said about those very people who during the severe years of the Great Patriotic War of 1941-1945 saved Europe from Nazism and total genocide, those same people who despite unskilled leaders during the stagnant years gathered 230 million tons of bread, mined 500 million tons of coal and produced 600 million tons of oil. And one does not have to be a great prophet to forecast with all reliability that the people can only be appeased when they see some sort of progress, some ray of hope in these drawn-out and tortuous days of social experiments.

Perestroika: The Betrayal of People's Hopes

There is something justified in the opinion that no matter how much we run down our democrats, they are the children of their time and cannot be otherwise, for in their very nature they are merely neo-Bolsheviks, only even more impudent. I agree to a great extent with these opinions, but I am convinced that this is not the gist of the matter. Yes, the people have become ensnared in a trap, become the victims of harsh times, this is now obvious, and their groan is even louder and more perceptible to those who have still not completely lost the ability to hear human suffering or forsaken their conscience. The overwhelming majority of people are keeping silent, although the impudence with which the so-called reform is being carried out and the essentially fantastical, nightmarish 50- and 100-fold rise in prices for life's essentials, bread, milk, sugar, tea, are insistently inciting people to protest, to feel discontent, to take action. But the people tolerate it. Why?

Due to apathy towards politics and politicians, due to their habit of long-suffering? Yes, this is all present, but, I repeat, it is not the gist of the matter. It is apparently in the fact that a great number of people continue to hope. For what? Ordinary people accepted perestroika (no matter how we desecrate it now, no matter how we speak of it, this is a fact), believed in it and continue to bear all the terrible adversities of today's difficult life, for they understand that it is impossible to turn back the clock. And no matter how the eloquent writers scare them, most people want neither chaos nor dictatorship, and this, obviously, is the main factor with which politicians have to reckon.

Ordinary people are placing increasing hope only on themselves. I had the opportunity to convince myself of this when visiting the Urals. I am not the first to note that returning to native environs after many years of absence is about as joyless as visiting old graveyards. I arrived in Magnitogorsk in the summer of 1992, eighteen years after I had left for Moscow and saw a different city and different people. The last decade, which has brought such radical changes, has altered the way of thinking and mood of the people.

I met and talked with a variety of people, institute researchers, employees of the Magnitostroy metallurgical works and trust, the intelligentsia and young businessmen... I wanted to understand what they thought and what concerned them, for the people of Magnitogorsk reflect to a great extent the opinion and mood of the entire province. I saw that the people of Magnitogorsk had maintained a sense of their own worth and were not embittered like the residents of the capital, having retained friendliness and genuineness in their relationships with each other. Most of the people I was able to talk with were indifferent to who is opposing whom in the central authorities and who is getting the better of whom. I clearly perceived the increasing indifference to the political spectacles of the executive and legislative powers which were so blatantly displayed in December 1992 at the Seventh Congress of the Russian People's Deputies. Magnitogorsk is openly placing hope on itself and certain that it will overcome the current difficulties.

During our conversations, my interlocutors openly said that they mainly relied on their own strength and were occupied primarily with their own personal concerns, building their dachas, expanding their orchards and vegetable gardens, creating their own business. Their main request was that the centre would not prevent people from relying on themselves and showing independence.

It was also noticeable, as it is in Moscow, that people not involved in production were in a much more difficult position: teachers, university professors, physicians and pensioners are distraught and confused and there is the obvious feeling of defencelessness among them. Many of them feel that nobody needs them and do not know where to turn for help. I doubt that we take this into consideration or understand it. And if we do not understand or take into consideration what the people of Magnitogorsk think or want, it will be difficult to hope for any rational solutions from the executive power.

What can help us in these hard times and where is our salvation? I think I am not alone when I repeat more and more frequently, like a prayer in times of hardship, during panic and strife, the destruction of culture and fall in morality, 'You alone are my hope, my source of faith and strength – my homeland.' We must admit that things are more painful and difficult for us today not just because of our wretched everyday lives, but because of the destruction of our homeland and the loss of the most important feeling which boosted our dignity, the feeling of belonging to a great power. The fall of the great power, its humiliating subordination to the western world and the begging in the church entrance for so-called humanitarian sops arouse in all honest people, and they are the overwhelming majority, a bitter, tear-biting sense of insulted national pride. How amazingly in tune with this national mood are the words of Alexander Blok: 'A country under the burden of insult and continuous violence, like a woman, loses her sense of shame, like an angel, droops its wings.'

This sense is intensified by the insistently violent and pointedly indiscriminate denial in the mass media of our past, to which a significant number of adult people are directly related whose mentality cannot accept these probings. Publicist Alexander Terekhov in the *Ogonyok* magazine (May 1992) noted very accurately: 'Under the deformations and distortions, and by imposing on the past and its bearers, on people of the older generation, contemporary ideas, which frequently only relate to a given moment, is tantamount to driving our own insanities and irrationalities into the grey heads of our fathers and grandfathers.'

In May 1992, Alexander Terekhov was still unaware of how at times the present insanities of society reverberate tragically in the grey heads of our veterans. In October 1992, yet another gravestone appeared in the Brest Fortress Memorial Complex, and not an anonymous one, but that of a participant in the bloody defence of Brest, in the 44th artillery regiment, Temiren Zimatov. Fifty years ago, this young defender of the Brest Fortress closely escaped a fascist bullet, but the current desperate days and the poverty and humiliation which our war veterans suffer proved too much for him. The heart of this front fighter could stand it no longer when he visited for the last time (he had done this for many years) the sacred place and saw what it had turned into; he committed suicide by throwing himself under a train.

Farewell notes do not lie. This is what the old soldier Zimatov wrote in his note: 'If I had died back then from my wounds I would have known that I had died for my country, but now I die from this wretched life.' In his letter the veteran asked to be buried on the ground he defended.

No matter how much our past is defiled, we remain an unusually rich country and our most important treasure is our history and our culture, our burial-mounds. Because of this we need to be extremely careful not to scatter to the wind the treasure which belongs to our homeland. I will present only two arguments to justify my opinion. I have already said that even in the recent, denied past, our state and government were not benefactors of culture, and such institutions as libraries, art galleries and museums were not particularly favoured by the authorities. But in 1992 an attempt was made to unabashedly pull apart and sell up museums with the government's blessing. The new draft of the government decree on museums, which did not contain any indication of the immunity of museum funds as national property, also failed to mention the state's obligation to protect and finance these national treasures. In his public statement, Academician Dmitry Likhachev called this draft a deliberate destruction of Russian culture and suggested bringing those who wrote it before an international court.

And another argument. Most reasonable people understood what the congress of USSR People's Deputies announced for March 17, 1992, after which the people's deputies themselves involuntarily subordinated themselves to the liquidation of the supreme parliamentary power of the Union. However, behind this outwardly absurd congress stood the attitude towards the most painful subject, the subject of the lost Homeland, the Union of Republics, which had lived as a single family through a difficult but long life, in which there had been disasters, but also joint victories. An expression of this national mood was also shown in the results of public opinion polls, and they are rather significant. According to the data of the Independent Institute of the Sociology of Parliamentarianism presented in *Izvestia* (March 16, 1992), the percentage of those in favour of holding a congress of USSR People's Deputies was 26 per cent, and those against 47 per cent. From any point of view, it is impossible to ignore the extremely significant number of supporters of the congress after all that had happened to it and the USSR People's Deputies.

I am convinced that the idea of protection of the homeland is capable of uniting the healthy forces of society and honest people regardless of their ethnic, religious or party affiliation. To prevent this protection from being lost in party and group declarations and the multitudinous wearisome speeches of politicians, it is necessary, in my opinion, to distinguish the main direction of activity (action instead of words) to save the country – the restoration of law and order, where both the official authorities with their administrative tools and broad circles of society could join forces. This is where it would be particularly beneficial today to hold meetings and demonstrations calling for the universal national repudiation of crime, corruption, legal debauchery and protection of the individual, family and children. And we should not be so quick to run down those public forces which have taken the first steps to join in the form of Russian patriotic associations and movements. The union of the national-patriotic movement with representatives of the Russian intelligentsia and socialist-oriented associations and groups is a force with which, in the very near future, if they keep their common sense, the authorities will have to reckon and achieve mutual understanding.

In the opinion of Academician Gennady Osipov, under the special, incomparable conditions of the former Union and the particular characteristics of most of the leaders (yesterday's communist party officials), an unusual deformation occurred at the practical level in the concept of democracy; it is reflected in the recognition of the absolute priority of the elected leaders of the legislative and executive powers, always expressing the will of the people and always right in their decisions and actions. In everything reigned the postulate: the elected leaders are always right, and their actions are always legal. In the face of this priority, competency, professionalism, experience and science are ignored.

I think that directly related to this is the appearance of such a progressive name as 'democrat' which many understand now as a term of abuse: the incontrovertible opinion of the leaders democratically elected but with authoritarian background who reform society solely in compliance with their own subjective ideas exults over everything. One of them absolutely determines what the press may or may not report, another states that he is the single head of the country and only at his kind disposal may ministers be appointed or dismissed or a particular question of the life of the people resolved or not resolved.

A second important indicator which demonstrates the political crisis is the absence in the powers-that-be of any sort of ideology. Apart from general words of becoming an enlightened Russia, they have nothing in the least intelligible to say. Whereas to the right are those who proclaim orthodoxy, monarchy and national tradition, and to the left those in favour of modernised slogans of a superpower, homeland and socialism, the attributes which they apparently retain for themselves are the market, democracy and capitalism. However, to the question of how he sees the future state structure, the Russian president replies: we are not building capitalism, but building a society in which people do not insult each other, steal, go on drinking binges or be lazy. In precisely the same way as the practice of humane socialism appeared impossible, it is also impossible to imagine humane capitalism, and real life today provides sufficient justification for such doubts. Under the new demototalitarianism, promises of a bright future are clearly in harmony with the demagogic propaganda which writes off every sin to the past authorities. The opinion is forming that in the ideological struggle, the current neodemocrats could not care less about what is Marxism and what orthodoxy, their only concern is to fill in the vacuum left in the place of former compulsory political education. And it is not surprising that the fathers of democracy and their followers, those who yesterday with books in hand prayed to Lenin, now for the sake of piety are swearing on the Bible.

A third indication that the political power crisis has reached its climax is that it is no longer possible for the leading circles to write off all the difficulties and blunders to their predecessors as they used to. In the eyes of most of the population, it is no longer possible to blame everything on the previously existing central legislative and executive powers of the USSR. Everyone is now clearly aware, as is demonstrated by the conclusion of the group of experts headed by Grigory Yavlinsky, that Russia's ruling authorities are responsible for the overwhelming destruction of the union state and have failed in their attempt to conduct the first stage of economic reform, for they have caused an increase in anarchy and the uncontrollability of the national economy and have accelerated the disintegration of Russia, while ethnic conflicts have developed into a state of war among the republics and nations.

The fourth indicator of the power crisis is that the authorities not only have failed to take any steps towards reaching a consensus in society, but, on the contrary, with an effort worthy of a better application, after taking up the momentum of destruction in August, 1991, have intensified to the limit the struggle among different political groups and parties, public movements and forces at all levels of power and in all regions. After the crushing defeat of the congress of people's deputies and the USSR Supreme Soviet and the sending into retirement of the USSR president, an intense, essentially continuous struggle has begun at all levels of legislative and executive power in Russia. This struggle reached a particularly critical point in December, 1992: the démarche of the Russian president in relation to the congress of people's deputies is convincing evidence of this.

A reflection of these processes is the critical situation in the political parties and public associations. An example is the split in *Democratic Russia*, a movement which was only recently so influential and which did not withstand the test of power. There is also the political and social situation in Moscow and St. Petersburg, the recent bastions of new democracy, where the leaders who came to power proved to be incapable of ruling. The appearance of a multitude of liberal, radical, patriotic, social democratic and other parties without any serious social support from below only confirms that at present the conditions for large political parties capable of functioning nationwide are lacking. The lack of trust from the population in the parties and public movements was blatantly expressed in 1992 in the unsuccessful attempt to create a broad centrist public association capable of heading the process of consolidation of healthy social forces in society under the banner of *The Movement of Democratic Reforms*.

Periodically conducted sociological surveys are also convincing proof of this. Here are some results of the poll conducted by the Independent Institute of the Sociology of Parliamentarianism on October 23, 1992. To the question, 'Are there any political organisations or movements in Russia which could reflect your personal opinion or principal position?', Muscovites responded as follows: 61% – there are none; 30% – no answer; and only 9% named political trends which they support.

Moreover, the critical situation in the country and the fall in prestige of the official authorities are arousing an insistent demand for new ways to stabilise the socio-political situation and the unification of people of good intention and common sense who represent different public movements and parties, support democracy and economic reforms and respond to the interests of the people.

Forecasts at such a difficult and contradictory time for the country can clearly not be favourable, for the events taking place frequently correspond neither to logic nor common sense. However, if we attempt to consider the possible development of political events based on the interests of the majority of the population (we admit that it is precisely these, the people's interests, which motivate the public process) and the real needs of society, we can, of course with no claims at absolute accuracy, provide some possible versions for stabilising the situation in the country and achieving a consensus in society.

Of indisputable interest is the growing influence of a block of public forces which represent the leading industrial enterprises of the country, in the form of a union called *Renewal*. The so-called Industrial Party, having created a strong *Civil Union* with the Democratic Party of Russia (Nikolai Travkin) and the National Party of Free Russia (Alexander Rutskoi) have serious reasons to claim a radical influence in society. This influence is determined by the real force and organisational ability of the personnel of the industrial enterprises which represent a significant part of the worker movement. This union has the prospect of strengthening ties with the regions of Russia and support from local authorities. The public prestige of this block and its potential for having real influence on the stabilisation of the political and economic situation in the country will to a great extent also depend on other important factors: the ability to attract the peasant movement to their side; the ability not to push aside but interact with socialists and communists in the form of those healthy forces and groups which have retained and enjoy support from below in many regions of Russia. No matter how events develop and opposition is manifested, the influence of the *Civil Union* on the formation and activity of the government following the 7th Congress of People's Deputies is bound to grow.

Chapter 7 – 'Thou Shalt Not Create Idols': The Tragedy of Gorbachev's Supporters

Forecasts and assessments of Russia's future and the way out of its current crisis constantly address the question of leadership: who is to blame for all our troubles? On whom now can we pin our hopes? It is usual to lament that many of our difficulties are due to the lack of new, talented, authoritative leaders.

One would be quite justified to say that only time and social necessity bring forth outstanding individuals: the era of Party hegemony, with its 'levelling down' (*uravnilovka*) and strict obedience, was not the most favourable for the appearance of talented figures able to take the helm and run the state. This was a period in which mediocrity was overwhelmingly to the fore. However, this theme demands separate and serious discussion. Here I wish only to touch on the question of why individuals who were so recently the object of enormous optimism can turn out to be bankrupt and suffer defeat.

The reader will have guessed that I am talking here about Mikhail Gorbachev. A great deal has been said and written about Gorbachev, and I can hardly lay claim to any new revelations. But people of my generation whose destinies were tied to his are duty-bound to state their opinion and sort out their own position, to assess their personal complicity and responsibility for what has happened to the country. Of course, I have in mind not an in-depth analysis of Gorbachev's actions and personal qualities, but merely the individual observations that go to make up an author's subjective point of view.

Life teaches us that every individual is allotted a role that depends on his personal qualities, on the times and conditions in which he lives and works. This is certainly the case with Mikhail Gorbachev. Everything he did was indeed conditioned by his personal qualities and by the times and conditions in which he lived.

Professor of psychology A. Belkin in the newspaper *Kultura* (Culture) of October 19, 1991, defines Gorbachev's character as narcissistic. Many of those who knew him would agree with this assessment, I believe. His dominant character traits were those of an individual mainly concerned with himself.

He was greatly affected by universal attention and public interest. He enjoyed the sense of his high calling, his status, his enormous power. This inner character that listened attentively only to himself combined with verbosity and an inability to listen to others. Gorbachev is part of that category of leaders who, even when they listen, do not hear good advice. As I know from my own experience, in personal conversations it was very hard to tell him anything. Furthermore, at the Central Committee secretariat, the Politburo and a multitude of other meetings he found it enormously difficult to listen to others.

In dealings with newspaper editors, figures from literature and the arts – a frequent occurrence in the early years of perestroika – his verbosity was particularly apparent. It was interesting to observe how, at the beginning of each meeting, Gorbachev would say that this time he had no intention of boring everyone with his own opinions and had come to listen closely to others' critical assessments of what was happening. However, his patience never lasted long. He soon forgot his opening words and the whole meeting would turn into an uninterrupted dialogue between him and anyone who spoke. Each time this scenario was repeated it met with greater and greater dissatisfaction and doubt as to the sincerity of his invitation to give expert advice.

Those who met him were particularly struck by Gorbachev's unnatural desire to please and produce a good impression. Sensitive to the impact of his speeches, he would sometimes see that he had spoken too much and, particularly early on, criticised his poor performances and talked about them openly, though he remained unable to change his ways.

People like Gorbachev, ambitious and overly self-opinionated, lack endurance and an ability to cope with setbacks. They are very vulnerable to defeat and failure. As the old saying goes, your successes reveal what you are capable of, and your failures show your worth. Convincing evidence of this unusual character evolution was Gorbachev's return from his Crimean dacha and appearance before the cameras after the coup attempt of August 1991. This was a different Gorbachev altogether: pale, confused, flustered, underconfident, it almost seemed that he had physically shrunk. This was the real worth of Gorbachev in crisis conditions.

The peculiarities of his character provide clues to many other questions about Gorbachev. Many of his critics accuse him of serious weakness in his inability to choose colleagues and assistants. I cannot agree with this. The issue was not ability or inability to choose: one cannot deny Gorbachev his clarity of vision, which was more than sufficient to enable correct judgement of an individual's merits. Here everything depended on approach, on the need to have strong figures nearby who in various spheres were better informed than he. Gorbachev simply denied this need for powerful figures with their own point of view (although he said much to the opposite effect). First and foremost in his immediate entourage he valued efficiency, obedience and respect.

People such as Gorbachev who are confident in their chosen status are rarely upset by or suffer from the departure of any particular individual from their team, since they feel no personal friendship or attachment. It was for this reason that he changed his close associates so painlessly and with such apparent ease.

Writers on Gorbachev often repeat the idea that his career was somehow unique. This opinion I share only in so far as it is not given to every peasant's son to run the state. I say this as a member of the same generation of children who tasted the bitter misfortune of the war and knew hard work, having seen their lives turned upside down. No matter how much we argue about it, the conviction of the 60s generation originated in the war, while our social formation as idealistic communists took place in the years of the Khrushchev thaw. Even here Gorbachev is far from unique. He is simply representative of his generation, with all its strengths and weaknesses.

One sometimes finds remarks concerning the influence on Gorbachev of people in various positions who were able to radically alter the formation and subsequent evolution of his ideas. Often included in their number is Alexander Yakovlev, a man of substantially greater experience than Gorbachev, especially in the international sphere. Yakovlev's influence is undeniable, and not on Gorbachev alone. But there is no need to oversimplify, as is often the case with hostile critics who purposefully exaggerate this influence and portray Gorbachev as nothing more than an obedient servant and populariser of others' ideas. Hostility does not help us reach an objective judgement. I believe that Gorbachev's views and ideas as he rose to power were the result of his own efforts and experience. I repeat: the origins of perestroika were in the 60s generation, in the times, in his village roots where pain and sorrow – I know this for myself – were more apparent and the deformity of Soviet life more obvious than in the city.

Gorbachev's career was clearly a result first and foremost of his personal qualities: he was undoubtedly an outstanding person. However, a major and sometimes determining factor was the Party system whose instrument he was. Moscow University opened the door to professional politics. His choice of career in the Komsomol was in no small measure a consequence of his return to his native region, where he was a well-known and accepted figure, now with a reasonable – by provincial standards – theoretical grounding. Knowing full well the possibilities open to him through the local Komsomol, he took a further step that was to affect his entire career, right up to his appointment in Moscow: he enrolled for evening classes and graduated from the agricultural institute.

I never worked in Komsomol organs, but my experience in Party committees allows me to conclude that many Komsomol functionaries at the time adopted some of the worst features of their Party higher-ups: kowtowing to bureaucratic rank, subservience and an ability to listen quietly to their superiors. In terms of their hypocrisy, the Komsomol apparatus – in particular its upper echelons – were not far behind the Jesuits.

The other stages in Gorbachev's political career were largely determined by the system of organisational work within the Party, a system that worked faultlessly and almost without interruption. His transition from Komsomol to the territorial party committee (*kraikom*) and on to his election as first secretary of the Stavropol city party committee was both logical and irresistible. The subsequent steps in his career were almost automatic: from second and then to first secretary of the CPSU territorial committee. His character as future Party leader was formed by the eight years he spent in the latter post, where he enjoyed unlimited power in the locality and universal subservience.

Gorbachev himself had a high opinion of his work as Party secretary for the Stavropol Territory. In an interview for *Nezavisimaya gazeta* he said, and not for the first time: 'I believe that I and my colleagues did much of interest in those conditions and cleared the road for many others.' I cannot help remarking, however, that those inhabitants of the Stavropol region to whom I have spoken have a somewhat more modest, if not sceptical, attitude to the activities of their first secretary. This is no mere coincidence, I believe, since all the personal features and qualities that made themselves known when Gorbachev became leader of Party and state were already fully formed and apparent in Stavropol: his almost nine-year stretch as first secretary provided all the conditions necessary for this to take place. Where many personal matters were concerned – individual appointments and so on – the first secretary of a regional committee had no less power than the Party leader. Incidentally, the image and habits of his wife Raisa, later to become well-known throughout the country, were also conditioned by life in good old Stavropol Territory, and her influence on her husband did not originate in Moscow.

The post of first secretary of a large regional committee opened up considerable possibilities in terms of a Party or state career. Furthermore, Stavropol and Krasnodar, being southern regions, were customary holiday locations for the top leadership, and there were therefore excellent opportunities for cultivating personal contacts.

I am describing all this in such detail because I want to convince the reader that there was nothing individually outstanding in Gorbachev's career: his rise to prominence was largely determined by the system in which repetition of previous behaviour was given preference over ideas. As for Gorbachev's appointment in 1978 to the Central Committee as secretary for agriculture after the death of V.D. Kulakov, I believe that it had little to do with any particular qualities he may have had as an agricultural specialist. One of the main factors was clearly the fact that the incumbent, Kulakov, had also been first secretary of the Stavropol territorial Party committee. This was also directly responsible for Gorbachev's rapid appointment as candidate member and then full member of the Politburo. The Party system was good at repeating the tried and tested.

Much has been written concerning the main reasons behind Gorbachev's appointment to General Secretary. There is a myth that it could have been otherwise, that Ligachev, Gromyko, Ryzhkov or others from among those involved in the decision could also have got the job. To the best of my knowledge this is also mere fantasy and conjecture. After Chernenko's death there was no other choice, nor could there have been. The system inside the Party was absolutely fixed and rigid: the man who was second to Chernenko in the Party, who chaired the meetings of the Central Committee secretariat and therefore ran the entire Party apparatus, and who conducted the Politburo meetings in the General Secretary's absence, was bound to take the latter's place. Thus Yuri Andropov, appointed by Brezhnev to run the Party apparatus after Suslov's death, in his turn became General Secretary. Konstantin Chernenko also assumed the post, though he was blessed with very limited personal and professional abilities, and his appointment was not only due to the fact that his weakness suited everyone else. It was he who ran the apparatus of the CPSU Central Committee, and given that Andropov did not have time before he died to transfer or dismiss him, Chernenko was simply doomed to lead the Party. Such were the strict and immovable canons of the Party system.

Writers on Gorbachev are frequently bewildered by his extraordinary popularity in the early stages of perestroika. We often forget that opinions of a person or event are always formed in comparison with previous figures and past events. Gorbachev's authority grew so fast because he seemed quite different to what we had been used to for so long under Brezhnev and Chernenko. His manner of speaking freely and naturally, his direct appeals to the people – this was all bound to bring him popularity and success. Of course, no less important was the content of what he had to say, and he said things that people had long been waiting to hear: we can't go on living like this, the Soviet people deserve a different, brighter future.

There is currently much discussion of the complexity and unpredictability of our people, how hard it is to get them moving in a new direction and to teach them different ways of living and working. But for some reason one rarely finds mention of people's naivety, their rapid acceptance of those who offer them a bright future, especially if it matches their own hopes and expectations.

There is much written on the theme of Gorbachev's 'mission', as though he represented the idealistic communists of the 1930s, many of whom were eliminated by Stalin, while the later generation was corrupted and demoralised by Brezhnev. I do not share this desire to portray Gorbachev as a prophet or messiah. In his very first actions and speeches as leader he said what had been expected ever since the 20th Party Congress and was inevitable once the generation of Brezhnev, Suslov, Chernenko and Gromyko had left the stage.

I cannot but agree (and Gorbachev said this himself on many an occasion) that he was a product of his generation and his time, and in his various doings he expressed all the latter's features and limitations. It was this, independent of psychological factors, that gave him his inconsistency and ambivalence. He wanted to be the great reformer, the leading democrat. But at the same time he wanted to remain national leader, head of Party and state, and to maintain the same authority, methods and relations with his close colleagues based on unquestioning obedience. This was the direct reason for Gorbachev's predilection for building palatial personal dachas, even at such a difficult time for the country. Visiting him in his Crimean dacha in Foros during the dramatic events of August 1991, his colleagues were first of all stunned by the luxury. Later they told trusted individuals that the Tsar himself hadn't lived as well as that.

In this respect I cannot help recalling a memorable trip abroad in December 1985, when I was still editor of *Sovetskaya Rossiya*. The Central Committee sent me as head of a party delegation to a conference of the Indian National Congress. The head of the party at the time was Indira Ghandi and its executive secretary was her son Rajiv, who had been to the USSR and was interested in the activities of the CPSU as ruling party. This, I believe, was the reason for our invitation to India. The conference took place in Calcutta from December 25 to 27. There were only half-a-dozen delegations from other countries, and we thus enjoyed considerable attention.

There were many meetings and conversations, one of which was particularly memorable: on December 26 I met and talked to Indira Ghandi. The conversation was unhurried, as is the custom in the East, and lasted over an hour, so I had the chance to take a close look at this remarkable woman and to ask her various questions. This was someone who was absolutely exhausted. Her face was pained and ascetic with large, lively eyes. Her entire appearance seemed to me to reveal a person fanatically devoted to her country and her people. I asked what it was that gave her the strength to endure such an enormous load, that kept her optimistic: after all, she would not live to see her country and its people prosperous and wealthy.

She looked at me closely and said that fate and her father had bequeathed her the destiny to be with her country through thick and thin, and that she would carry her cross right to the end. As for the question of whether or not she would live to see her people prosper, she understood that this could not be, that life is short. But she would follow the road that leads to human happiness, and after her there would come her son. Fate indeed decided that her time was short: the following year she was murdered.

Why have I recalled this meeting? Because at a crucial time for our society the leadership of Party and state lacked the same fanaticism and devotion to their country and its people. As someone once remarked: under Brezhnev the Party leadership was well-off, formless and complacent and became a leadership of second home-owners (*dachniki*), concerned mainly with their own comfort and well-being. Gorbachev also had features of a Party leader in this mould.

He was reluctant to risk or part with the attributes of Party and state power. While talking about democracy and coming out for electoral reform, which led to the first ever contested elections in the history of the USSR, he himself did not want to be elected as a people's deputy, but was instead selected at a Central Committee plenum. This was seen by many as an example of his inconsistency.

Gorbachev had a second chance to break out of the traditional role of leader appointed from above when it came to the Union presidency. At the beginning of 1990 he could still have won support for free elections to this post. The decision would have been a risky one, but victory, which was still very much on the cards, would have had tremendous consequences both for him and the USSR. But he was frightened and confined himself to the Congress of People's Deputies. It marked the beginning of the gradual end to his influence, popularity and authority. Evidence of this was the result of the presidential vote, which was very different from that by which he was elected Chairman of the Supreme Soviet. This was the inevitable price of indecision, timidity and delay in taking constructive decisions, especially those concerning burning social questions such as the economy and ethnic relations, where his incompetence was particularly obvious.

To this day the debate continues in the press over why Gorbachev's popularity in the West, which remains high, was so unstable and short-lived in his native country. To me the answer is obvious: the consequences of his reforms were enormous, especially from the Western point of view. The great stand-off between the two superpowers, each armed with weapons that endangered the whole world, collapsed, as did the mighty Warsaw Pact and the entire world system of socialist states.

This change in the climate of relations gave hope to the peoples of many different nations that the danger of world war was over. People in Europe, America and Asia made a direct connection between this and the name of Mikhail Gorbachev. However, the results of his foreign policy received a far more contradictory reception domestically, for the price to be paid was too high: the collapse of the USSR, the destruction of the army, the transformation of a mighty global state into a territorial conglomerate, battered and torn by internal conflicts and contradictions. The slump of this once great power to the level of pitifully seeking foreign aid weighs heavy on the hearts of all who hold our Fatherland dear.

I will also presume to suggest that the results of Gorbachev's foreign policies were not the only reason for his falling popularity at home. Soviet citizens were able to watch Gorbachev at far closer quarters over a considerable period and could observe his evolution from new and innovative behaviour, policies, speeches and promises to repeating what he had said three years ago. Attitudes to the new and innovative gradually hardened as the promised changes were delayed and people's hopes were not realised. I have no intention of offending Mikhail Gorbachev, but one might compare all this with attitudes to an actor who can only play one role, that of the hero, i.e. the one who knows how to look better than he is in reality and to promise more than he can really deliver. The audience for this one-man-show was different in the West: they saw this talented actor only once or twice, and he created an impression because he broke the usual patterns of behaviour for Soviet leaders. As time passed and the economic and political crisis grew, the Soviet audience found this political theatre with its single actor in the role of hero and national saviour less and less convincing. In 1990 Gorbachev's travels and encounters within the country were already running into problems. By the following year they had become altogether impossible: people not only refused to listen, but he deeply annoyed them.

Drawing historical analogies is a risky business, since they are usually determined by the author's subjective interpretation. This is inevitable, since history and people's actions in different epochs never repeat themselves exactly. Herzen was right when he remarked: 'History never returns, she has no need for her old frocks.' But at the same time analogies are useful and necessary to highlight an individual's features and to assess his achievements through the prism of time.

I say all this because I was struck by Victor Bondarev's remarks in the magazine *Rodina* (Motherland) in his article *Kerensky and Gorbachev: Two Epochs and Two Dramas* (No. 9, 1992). Bondarev notes the similarity in the events and in the destinies of their main protagonists during Russia's great historical dramas at the beginning and end of the twentieth century. In each case there was economic collapse, crisis, the total impoverishment of the population, mass suffering and bloodshed, an orgy of separatism and so on. Bondarev believes that Kerensky was the only leader in Russia's history who tried to achieve democracy by legal means: in this he sees Gorbachev as Kerensky's one and only successor. There is much in common in terms of the scale of their achievements and the tragedy of their fates. Lastly, they are also united in their tendency to compromise and their constant efforts to occupy the centrist middle ground: while Kerensky balanced between Lenin and Kornilov and in 1918 took up the famous slogan of the Socialist Revolutionaries, 'Neither Lenin nor Kolchak!', Gorbachev manoeuvred first between the Party reformers and conservatives, then between the Communists and the so-called democrats, and finally between the sovereign republics and the centre. According to his contemporaries, the paradox of Gorbachev's centrism is that as Soviet president he managed both to head the state and the opposition at one and the same time.

How strange that August should have been a fatal month in the lives of both Gorbachev and Kerensky: August was the month of the Kornilov uprising of 1917 and the coup attempt of 1991. To this day uncertainty remains as to Kornilov's intention to seize power, and the strange behaviour of the 1991 coup leaders also raises major doubts concerning whether or not this was a genuine putsch, whether it involved the entire leadership with the sole exception of the president.

Bondarev's conclusions are as interesting as they are debatable: namely, that Kerensky started the second revolution while Gorbachev completed it, that the former's fate is well known while the latter is sure of the gratitude of history if his perestroika finally leads to the return of one-sixth of the world's land surface to modern civilisation. On the other hand, Bondarev argues, if it ends with a social catastrophe and the loss of millions of lives, then Gorbachev will become Russia's 'Kerensky mark II'. These are doubtful conclusions indeed, since we know full well that it was not Kerensky who began the second revolution and it was not Gorbachev who completed it. Bondarev admits this himself when he talks about the danger of social catastrophe. But a catastrophe has already taken place, thousands of innocent people have died, millions have been impoverished and made outsiders in their own home country.

The features of Gorbachev's personality and behaviour I observed at close quarters in one of the fields that caused him the most unpleasantness: the mass media, i.e. radio, television and the press. The many years of Central Committee meetings, and occasionally the Politburo, that he chaired, his frequent meetings with newspaper editors, the heads of Gosteleradio, TASS and APN, individual encounters and telephone conversations, particularly during the period of my work in Soviet television – all this enabled me to form an impression of Gorbachev, to give my own opinion and assessment of his achievements. What I have to say about him is largely the result of my own observations, and not what I have read elsewhere. It is thus a subjective opinion and cannot lay claim to the whole truth.

Gorbachev's ambivalence and contradictions were perhaps most clearly expressed in his relations with the press and with those whom he appointed to run it.

The logic of political development at the time meant that the press, radio and television were at the sharp end of the changes under way throughout the country. I admit that we the editors were most inspired by the General Secretary's attention, by our frequent meetings and conversations and the position that he adopted. I remember one of our early encounters at the beginning of 1986, when glasnost in the media was taking its first steps. Talking about the role of the mass media, Gorbachev developed an interesting and, for us, most unexpected idea. He argued that many features of our conservatism, our mistakes and miscalculations – the source of stagnation in the Party's ideas and policies – were a consequence of the lack of opposition and alternative points of view. At the current stage of development of our society, he argued, the press could become an opposition of this original type. For us, brought up on a diet of subservience and constant pressure from the Central Committee apparatus, this was indeed a major innovation.

Taking Gorbachev's words seriously as the genuine advent of glasnost, media editors began all the more actively to play the role of opposition to the official policies of Party and government. The incidence of conflicts between Party committees and the media increased. At Central Committee plenums republican leaders and regional secretaries firmly demanded that a stop be put to this wave of criticism in the press. In our speeches at meetings of this sort, I and my colleagues had to argue in our defence that criticism was the best means of assisting perestroika by revealing the most immediate signs of sickness in society and demanding that the Party surgically intervene in the healing process.

I have to agree that Gorbachev's views and his attitude to the press, especially in his first two or three years as General Secretary, largely determined its critical orientation and its growing activity in all spheres of social life. The press was indeed forging ahead, playing the role of reconnaissance, clearing the obstacles from the path of the main battalions and picking the targets for perestroika's main offensives. I have already mentioned that there was no shortage of mistakes and subjectivism on the part of journalists who wanted a special place in society, yearning to be the bearers of truth and the only sphere beyond criticism.

However, perestroika's constructive projects suffered defeat after defeat. Social tensions increased, ethnic conflicts grew and all the more frequently voices in the press began to ask: are we really going in the right direction? Has the commander really planned a clear route? By now it was clear that pluralism was not merely an exercise in polemics, but the expression of different interests and positions in a struggle for power. To the extent of all this, so the inconsistency in Gorbachev's decisions and policies, including his attitude to the press, began to make itself felt. He continued to talk about glasnost and pluralism, maintaining his image as a consistent democrat, but in his deeds he revealed a growing displeasure with the press, in particular when he himself was directly concerned.

It was then, in 1989, that he began the strange conflict with V. Starkov, editor of *Argumenty i fakty* (Arguments and Facts). In the best traditions of the CPSU General Secretary of old he demanded the latter's resignation, charging the propaganda department with the task of making sure this took place. In the meantime the editorial staff of the paper, which was published by the independent *Znanie* (Knowledge) all-Union society, decided that Gorbachev's decision was a case of Party treachery and refused to let their editor go. The development of this conflict caused a storm of public opinion and was effectively the first instance of Gorbachev's public disgrace;

it did him a lot of damage in the eyes of those who liked and sincerely supported him. This is but one small detail revealing Gorbachev's real nature, his ambivalence, his lack of sincerity and consistency, without which it was hard to believe his words and intentions as head of state.

In saying this I have no intention of denouncing Gorbachev or showing his blacker side. Anyone can see that there is no longer any particular need: the citizens of our land have long since made up their minds about Gorbachev and nothing can now be changed. My remarks serve the purpose of generalising my own observations and opinions about a man who, without any doubt, left his mark on the country's history.

Whilst everywhere proclaiming and defending democratic reforms, Gorbachev was unable inwardly to overcome the national leader within him – he had too great a faith in his omnipotence and preeminence. He never fully understood that it was impossible to halt the ideas that he himself had announced and scattered on the fertile soil of a country that had for so long awaited national revival. He could not grasp that, with glasnost proclaimed as official state policy and reinforced in parliamentary law, the media could no longer live and work according to the old ways, that they could not be treated like before, permitting one thing and forbidding another.

At the risk of repeating myself, I shall state once again that Gorbachev and his immediate entourage (including both his sincere supporters and those whose job it was to work with him) did not understand that one cannot simply curb the television. The latter is nonetheless a powerful and influential medium, even if it sometimes voices extreme opinions and is monopolised by certain groups. It was impossible to treat television and its employees as they had been treated in the not-so-distant past, i.e. to run the show as though it was an army, keep it in a tight grip and issue top-down commands right and left. Neither Nenashev, Kravchenko nor Yakovlev could do anything to improve television while the people above us remained set in their ways, while there was no mechanism to bring about the real dependence of television not on the government or the Party, but on the people itself, the viewers.

Gorbachev talked endlessly about 'the new thinking' and new

approaches, and one has to admit that he largely convinced us that he was right. One of his favourite phrases was: 'One cannot introduce new policies and start afresh using old methods and means.' But he himself, even more so than others, maintained the distance of an old-style commander, manager and leader, especially in his relations with the media. He talked about new thinking and new relationships, but kept up the usual arbitrary, administrative approaches and attitudes. He was scared to rely on people who believed in him and were ready to follow his ideas but were reluctant to be his unthinking servants as before.

Gorbachev could not understand that people believed and applied his ideas, which thereby became a reality and created a new way of living, a different system of interpersonal relationships independent of the rung of the social ladder. In these conditions, perhaps for the first time, he inevitably became subject to these new attitudes, to the newly open and direct pressure and influence of public opinion and the unstable mood of the crowd. The press was and remained merely an instrument that reflected changing opinion, and by the logic of the process (everything in this world has a consequence) it began to attack the very person who had done more than anyone else to make it free and independent.

Journalists today are raising the question of Gorbachev's possible return to power. This is no mere caprice: Gorbachev himself has frequently addressed this theme. Thus he told the *Berliner Zeitung* in March 1992: 'The country needs me. I can sense it. Many people, in particular the intelligentsia, are changing their minds about me. They understand me better.' A month later he referred – surely no accident – to the political career of de Gaulle, who after his resignation returned to the political stage as president of France. His forecasts concerning Russia's political future are becoming all the more frequent and confident. Commentators believe that these elements go to form a whole and reflect Gorbachev's intention to return to political power. Is this a real possibility?

The country is indeed in a crisis situation and we are close to a social explosion. Consequently, a change of government and leadership is probable. Could Gorbachev be involved? Undoubtedly his political experience as the man who began the changes, and his opinions and judgement concerning the current situation, are a fact of political life. There is much in this, however, that is the result of inertia, a nostalgia for the recent past engendered by a growing antipathy to the course adopted by the current leadership. In answering this question it seems to me that the most sensible approach is to start from the attitudes to Gorbachev of the main social and political forces on which the country's political future depends. There is *Renewal*, the so-called Industrial Party, representing the interests of practical men backed by big industry. The influence of this lobby is quite likely to grow. However, one should not over-estimate the extent of sympathy for Gorbachev among industrial managers closely linked to the regional administrative leaderships. They well remember how the destruction of the country's economy began.

Also growing in influence is the group of organisations and movements uniting national-patriotic forces under the flag of national salvation. The national-patriots sharply condemn Gorbachev for his helpless and ineffective attempts to save the Soviet Union and the highly contradictory results of his foreign policy, which resulted in national humiliation.

Of late there has been a notable consolidation of social forces with a socialist orientation. The influence of the communists is growing, brought together as they are in various groupings and combinations. The catastrophic worsening of social conditions in the country and the universal poverty, together with the trial of the CPSU before the Constitutional Court, has undoubtedly stimulated a growth in the influence and consolidation of forces with a socialist orientation. The name Gorbachev is anathema within this movement, and this opinion of the former General Secretary is unlikely to change. If one can be tolerant and level-headed concerning such an unexpected evolution in the views and convictions of our former Party leader, there are also moral norms and rules of behaviour, and here it is impossible to defend Gorbachev and his actions.

Finally, one should add that many of the steps taken by Gorbachev after his resignation have lowered his authority even further. His extraordinarily energetic and frantic attempts to raise money for the Gorbachev Foundation in Germany, Japan, the USA, Israel, South America and elsewhere have not helped to raise his popularity or increase people's faith in him. His monthly trips abroad, the millions of dollars in royalties – whether real or exaggerated by the press – only serve to irritate our impoverished countrymen, many of whom see them as a reward for services rendered in the past in the business of dismantling the Soviet Union and destroying a mighty superpower. Even his criticisms of the current leadership, which are justified in many ways, have not enabled him to regain the people's trust. His opinions and forecasts win him favour neither in ruling circles nor among ordinary people, for both continue to believe that the origins of the current catastrophe lie in the incompetence of the former Soviet president, that it is he who was the originator of so much trouble and misfortune for us all.

Gorbachev's energetic attempts through his contacts with the mass media to present an image of a politician with big potential more often than not have had the opposite effect. Here one should not forget that there is a great difference between the analyses and opinions of a head of state, the legitimate representative of his country and its policies, and an ordinary person, even if he is an experienced politician (not to mention the inevitable affect of the political reputation of a defeated ex-president). Judging by his speeches and interviews in the press, radio and television, it seems to me that Gorbachev has still not recognised or understood this difference. Otherwise it is hard to explain his hasty agreement to become a freelance correspondent for several western newspapers and his overly numerous and tiresome appearances in the Russian media, just like before. In this connection, a sensible politician who is favourably disposed towards Gorbachev once remarked to me that a man who loses power and so rapidly becomes a newspaper and TV commentator cannot possibly lay claim to be a future president.

The above remarks enable the reader to assess my opinion of Gorbachev, whether or not they agree with it. But the question, to which I am obliged to answer, remains: who has the right to judge?

This is no easy matter, but I shall say what I think. Neither I nor others like me can pass judgement on Gorbachev. Together with him we bear the responsibility for what happened in the country: for the death of the Soviet state, the collapse of industry and the economic catastrophe that is now a fact of life, for the impoverishment and humiliation of the population, for moral and spiritual decay and for the rise in crime. And whatever each of us thinks about his own part in perestroika and however he judges his own blame, whatever justification he might seek, however hard he may try to distance himself from Gorbachev – for us there can be no leniency nor forgiveness for all that we have brought upon our country and its people.

Of course, each can judge and punish himself according to his own honour and conscience. All the same, with what anguish did Tvardovsky once write:

> *I know no guilt*
> *That they from battle did not return,*
> *That young and old*
> *They stayed forever, the point is not*
> *Who I could have saved, who could I not,*
> *That's not the point; but could I, could I, could I...?*

I cannot judge, because I believed then as I believe now (and I can vouch for the fact that this is not my personal opinion alone) that the reforms begun in 1985 were inevitable and irreversible because objective laws were being broken; they were a natural development, to the path of which we were bound to return. Whatever its outcome, we are all – including its opponents today – a product of perestroika, and Gorbachev, whatever judgement we might make of him, will go down in history as a reformer who not only grasped the necessity of radical social reform but who also had the courage to begin it. Moreover, all those of us who consider ourselves idealistic communists, who anticipated and worked for reform and who welcomed perestroika as their goal in life, we served not Gorbachev, but the great popular cause in which we believed. Thus I cannot agree with those who now regret their former faith in Gorbachev and who see him as a fatal error, a dreadful mistake. Maybe for some this will be hard to stomach, but they sound to me like the embittered servant whom his master has cast aside.

I understand that it is hard for us, Gorbachev's associates, to see how fate played such a cruel joke by giving us so weak and helpless a man for leader at such a major turning point. It does not help to reflect on whether or not there are satanic origins to our misfortune, brought upon our fallen and sinful world by the Evil Spirit; on whether or not Gorbachev's mission in our country was to serve the will of the Evil Spirit in his role as 'prince of darkness'.

The desire to explain away all our troubles in terms of their other-worldly origins can only comfort but not alleviate our citizens' misfortune, because then we'll have to wait till doomsday for the people's liberation from this power of darkness.

Neither do I share the opinion of those who, while free of superstition, try to explain our tragedy as simply the result of Gorbachev's evil will. In this regard the honest account by Yegor Ligachev in his book *The Gorbachev Enigma* is yet one more confirmation of the tragedy and responsibility of Gorbachev's supporters, who at a crucial historical juncture were unable to change the course of events and who were therefore helpless hostages of harsh times, subservient cogs in the Party machine. As a well-known Oriental saying goes: 'In a flock of sheep the scapegoats are always the most stupid.' And thus we, Gorbachev's colleagues, were held up as scapegoats before the public. And it serves us right, for we are only reaping what we sowed, and we cannot complain.

I am not motivated by any resentment of Gorbachev – and that goes for this book as well. I am the author and I answer for my own actions and convictions, I am mercilessly self-critical and do not hide my responsibility before my country. I repeat, Gorbachev's mistakes, miscalculations, false starts, his personal qualities and achievements – these are not for me and those like me to judge. Of this I am convinced, for I stick to a rule that must be observed by anyone who wants to maintain his self-respect: namely, that our criteria for judging social phenomena and other individuals are essentially expressions of our own personal inclinations. In everyday language this is properly called the right to judge others according to one's own standards. Given that this is so, I and the others around Gorbachev were duty bound to have criticised him at the time when his personal limitations were already clear, at least in outline: his inability to run the country roused to opposition, his bewilderment that perestroika had provoked unexpected and unpredictable social and ethnic conflicts, which grew at an unbelievable pace and which he had neither the ability nor the strength to stop. It was then in 1989-90 that I and other Gorbachev supporters on the Central Committee and in the government should have stood up and said clearly: we have begun the great task of social renewal, but the experience of the last three years shows that we don't understand our main aims, we don't have a clear view of the way forward and, particularly dangerous, we don't know the country and its people as well as we should. But instead both we and Gorbachev comforted ourselves with phrases such as: 'The main thing is to get stuck in, and then we'll see'; or 'We are learning together with perestroika, with each new stage we are enriching our experience and ability.'

We had the chance to express all our doubts and anxieties at Central Committee plenums: I myself often spoke and said much that was unpleasant for the Party leadership to hear. But clearly I was not sufficiently persuasive and did not say everything that needed to be said. This self-limitation was not through fear – there was already nothing to be afraid of – but more from the habit of hoping that the people who stood one step higher up knew better how to proceed in those difficult times. There were, however, those among us who indeed got up at conferences, congresses and plenums and said that we had started our journey with neither a map nor a fixed route, and that we had only a vague idea of where we were going and where we would end up. But they won no support from the Central Committee, the government or the people's deputies.

How odd that Gorbachev should still be denying this and accusing people of stupidity for saying that we began perestroika without a thorough programme! This is typically inconsistent on his part. Thus in an interview in *Nezavisimaya gazeta* in August 1992 he said, and not for the first time: 'I do not believe anyone who says that such a reform project, such a big idea, could have been immediately worked out in all its details: there were so many factors that even the biggest super-computer could not cope with them all. Each of these factors was enormous, starting from the size of the country right through to the nature of this society and the number of different peoples inhabiting it.'

Gorbachev's inconsistency is particularly striking when one analyses the evolution of his views regarding socialism: from orthodox to social-democratic to a complete hotchpotch in the form of the so-called 'new civilisation'. Furthermore, at each of these stages he never omitted to present his latest shift as a deeply-held conviction. His interview in *Nezavisimaya gazeta* mentioned above was no exception. In order that the reader may get an idea of one of the latest of Gorbachev's 'deeply-held convictions', I shall cite him at length: 'I believe that the orientation on building a society of the socialist type, a socialist formation, was mistaken. We must move on to a new civilisation in which there will be different ideas – liberal, conservative and socialistic, together with general human values. This is my deeply-held conviction.' One cannot resist citing the ancients on this question: 'There is no greater misfortune than when a person begins to fear that the truth will reveal him for what he is.'

Only time and the people, who have become the object of perestroika and its hostages, will be the judge of Mikhail Gorbachev. The time will come when today's opinions will be free of strong emotion, resentment and passing bias, when it will be possible to give an objective assessment of his role in the history of our country. The people in their turn will reveal their inherent wisdom and, based on their practical experience, will rightly judge the results of the changes that he began and the price that was paid for them.

I understand that I cannot avoid the question: are these remarks for the better, is it right to criticise the fallen? I believe that they are indeed for the better, since I admit that I offer them to the reader not merely as a confession but also for the edification of my contemporaries, especially those who came after us. And they need it – if the course of events in the country at present and their tendency to repeat themselves is anything to go by.

Throughout our lives we are cautioned by the commandment: 'Thou shalt not create idols.' But nonetheless we refuse to learn from history, we take nothing from the wisdom of the past. Everything only repeats itself. Every time a new figure comes to power he begins with merciless criticism of the past, exposing its aristocratic privileges and caprices. But time passes and everything comes full circle, only on a higher level corresponding to the new conditions. Why? Is it merely because human weakness is so great and the demands of power and glory so hard to withstand? No, this is not the only reason. We have long known that it is the court that makes the king, and that it does so skilfully and irreversibly. It is time for us to admit (time is passing, yet still I see no admissions) that it was we, Gorbachev's close associates – who therefore still don't have the right to judge him – who did everything possible to ensure that his deeds and attitudes reiterated the features common to old leaders of the past – the past that we had all rejected. We made of him an idol just like all the rest.

I am writing these remarks not in the wake of the past, but in anticipation of the future. As I walk to the metro along the Rublevs-koye Shosse, a huge cavalcade of black ZIL limousines roars past at enormous speed, while far ahead, stopping everything in its tracks, is an outrider from which a ruthless voice booms – just like under the Tsar, only through a loudspeaker: down on your knees, citizen, tremble before the leadership. Everything is repeating itself.

I shall end my remarks on Gorbachev without fear of repeating what I said at the beginning. Everyone has a part to play in life, depending on one's character and strength of will, one's personal abilities and moral qualities, on the times and conditions in which one is fated to make one's way, and also, more likely than not, on destiny, which is determined for each of us on a higher plane. Gorbachev's role was merely to begin the transformation of our country: he was neither granted the time nor the strength and ability to do more. He couldn't cope with the storm that he brought forth. These elemental forces were stronger, and he himself was more of a preacher and enlightener than a wise and experienced politician, a head of state that could match the scale of this great country and be able to stand firm among the heaving waves of change.

Other books from Open Gate Press:

The Social History of the Unconscious
by George Frankl

in 2 paperback volumes:

Vol. 1 Archaeology of the Mind
ISBN 1 871871 16 6 p/b £8.95 232pp

In this book, Frankl applies the techniques of psychoanalysis to recent archaeological findings to trace the psychological development of humanity. His method enables us to gain a new understanding of how the mind originated, how our earliest ancestors became toolmakers, and how cultures developed. We are shown the conflict between matriarchy and patriarchy, and above all, the nature of patriarchal paranoia, that fatal disease which was and continues to be the source of warfare.

His conclusions are bound to transform some of our fundamental concepts about our social existence.

Vol. 2 Civilisation: Utopia and Tragedy
ISBN 1 871871 17 4 p/b £8.95 256pp

With this volume we enter history and, in particular, the history of Western civilisation. Through his examination of the unconscious driving forces which produced the great ideas of monotheism, Greek philosophy, democracy and scientific reasoning, Frankl enables us to gain important insights into the conflicts of civilisation and its failures to fulfil its aspirations. By its world-wide influence, the West has assumed an unprecedented responsibility for humanity everywhere, and indeed, for the survival of the planet. But in order to meet those responsibilities, we have to understand the causes of our failures.

The scholarship is prodigious ... today and for the first time I have been properly introduced to my ancestors. Dr. Peter Randell

One takes it almost for granted that Frankl writes with great intellectual power and lucidity, but it is his generosity and kindness which I find particularly impressive. Prof. Eva Wolf, Vienna University

For me, this book has joined that group of books which make for compulsive reading – a book that is difficult to put down until it has been read from cover to cover – and one which should be in every doctor's personal library.
Dr. Philip Hopkins, Journal of the Balint Society

A learned, carefully argued book which should be read by anyone interested in the humanities. Prof. Paul Kline, British Journal of Medical Psychology

The Unknown Self

by George Frankl

ISBN 1 871871 05 5 h/b £16.50   ISBN 1 871871 18 2 p/b £7.95   240pp

This book is based upon Frankl's observations as a psychoanalytic therapist over a period of some thirty-five years.

He began his psychoanalytic work in what would nowadays be called the 'classical' mould of psychoanalysis, but extended and deepened Freud's concepts, opening up new dimensions of the psyche which were not accessible to the pioneers. His method of hypnoid analysis makes it possible for patients to remember and to re-live some of the long-forgotten experiences of their lives, expanding the boundaries of our understanding of the unconscious mind. *The Unknown Self* traces the psychological development of individuals from early infancy, and shows how a wide range of neurotic and psychotic conflicts originate It combines rigorous scholarship with a deep humanity, which will enable the reader to experience illuminating moments of self-recognition and provide a new understanding of the often baffling behaviour of children.

The Unknown Self *is, quite simply and without unnecessary hyperbole, stupendous! I have never read anything so penetrating and enlightening.*
Dr. Edward Roth

... profound insights, humanity and passion.
Stephen Davy, *Oxford Times*

Exploring the Unconscious

by George Frankl

ISBN 1 871871 06 9 h/b £12.95 ISBN 1 871871 07 7 p/b £7.95   184pp

An exposition of the clinical methods developed by George Frankl, this book is the third volume in the series *Psychoanalysis and Society*. The reader is invited into the psychoanalytic laboratory – the consulting room – to witness how the patient is led to reveal to himself as well as to the analyst the secret world of his unconscious mind.

This book opens a whole new chapter in the study of the unconscious. Frankl has developed a new method of psychoanalytic therapy which enables the patient actually to re-experience the traumatic situations which were responsible for the formation of his neurotic symptoms; the patient is enabled to understand how his neurosis has developed and to adopt fresh attitudes which are in keeping with his desire for health and self-fulfilment.

It is essential reading for practitioners of psychotherapy and those who are concerned with mental health, for it provides new insights into the unconscious areas of the mind, and sets new standards of psychoanalytic efficiency.

The Entangled Civilization:
Democracy, Equality, and Freedom at a Loss
by Dr Michio Kitahara
ISBN 1 871871 23 9 380pp hb £24.95

Why are democracy, equality and freedom currently in such turmoil? Kitahara discusses the confusion and pessimism in Western civilization today. The author presents his theory of civilization and suggests how the enormous problems within Western civilisation can be addressed by pursuing the original basis of Western civilization, individualism. The three key values of democracy, equality and freedom are then re-interpreted from the perspective of individualism and possibilities for dealing with the problems of Western civilization are suggested.

Michio Kitahara received his PhD from the University of Uppsala, Sweden, in 1971. He held teaching or research appointments at the Universities of Maryland, Michigan and San Francisco, as well as at the State University of New York at Buffalo. He is currently Director of the Nordenfeldt Institute, Gothenburg, Sweden.

Previous publications include five books, of which the most recent are *Children of the Sun: The Japanese and the Outside World*, New York: St Martin's Press, 1989, and *The Tragedy of Evolution: The Human Animal Confronts Modern Society*, NewYork, Praeger, 1991. He has also published 55 articles in professional journals in the USA and Europe.

The Characters of Theophrastus
ISBN 1 871871 11 5 150pp pb £7.95

Theophrastus, the first great psychologist, pupil of Aristotle and heir to the Lyceum, was known by the title *divine speaker* because of his powers of observation and eloquence. We are shown thirty character types depicted with masterly insight, and a reading of the book soon reveals that human nature has changed little over the last two millennia; indeed, it is this which gives the *Characters* the status of a classic. This translation, reproduced in facsimile from an edition of 1831, contains a large number of beautiful line engravings of the characters observed.

Garganette:The Amazing Story of a Giant Female
by Saba Milton
ISBN 1 871871 09 3 152pp h/b £7.95

A charmingly profound, beautifully written and delightfully funny account of the early life of a descendant of Rabelais' Gargantua.

Saba Milton writes far, far better than most humorous writers ... she has a most unusual sense of rhythm so that her sentences build up a momentum, and flow onward quite beautifully ... brilliant dialogue.   John Cleese

DATE DUE

HIGHSMITH #45230

Printed in USA